THOMAS COOK
Travellers

LOIRE VALLEY

BY
KATHY ARNOLD AND PAUL WADE

Produced by AA Publishing

Written by Kathy Arnold and Paul Wade
Original photography by Bob Moore

Edited, designed and produced by AA Publishing.
© The Automobile Association 1996.
Maps © The Automobile Association 1996.
Reprinted June 1996.

Distributed in the United Kingdom by AA
Publishing, Norfolk House, Priestley Road,
Basingstoke, Hampshire RG24 9NY.

A CIP catalogue record for this book is available
from the British Library.

ISBN 0 7495 1019 6

The contents of this publication are believed correct at the time of
printing. Nevertheless, the publishers cannot accept responsibility for any
errors or omissions, or for changes in the details given in this guide, or
for the consequences of any reliance on the information provided by the
same. Assessments of attractions, hotels, restaurants and so forth are
based upon the author's own experience, and therefore descriptions
given in this guide necessarily contain an element of subjective opinion
which may not reflect the publisher's opinion or dictate a reader's own
experiences on another occasion.
**We have tried to ensure accuracy in this guide, but things do
change and we would be grateful if readers would advise us of any
inaccuracies they may encounter.**

Published by AA Publishing (a trading name of Automobile Association
Developments Limited, whose registered office is Norfolk House,
Priestley Road, Basingstoke, Hampshire RG24 9NY. Registered number
1878835) and the Thomas Cook Group Ltd.

Colour separation: BTB Colour Reproduction, Whitchurch, Hampshire.

Printed by Edicoes ASA, Oporto, Portugal.

Cover picture: *Chambord, largest of all the Loire châteaux*
Title page: *Château de Sully*
Above: *Hôtel de Ville, Loches*

Contents

About this Book

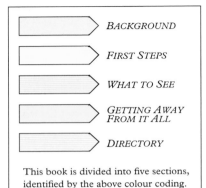

BACKGROUND

FIRST STEPS

WHAT TO SEE

GETTING AWAY
FROM IT ALL

DIRECTORY

This book is divided into five sections,
identified by the above colour coding.

Swinging in Chinon: the Medieval
Market in August

Background gives an introduction to
the region – its history, geography,
politics, culture.

First Steps offers practical advice on
arriving and getting around.

What to See is an alphabetical listing of
the places to visit, interspersed with
walks and tours.

Getting Away From it All highlights
places off the beaten track where it's
possible to relax and enjoy peace and
quiet.

Finally, the **Directory** provides practical
information – from shopping and
entertainment to children and sport.
Special highly illustrated features on
specific aspects of the region appear
throughout the book.

BACKGROUND

'If Paris is France's head,
Orléans is its heart.'
OLD SAYING

Introduction

*T*he Loire Valley is one of the world's prime tourist attractions, its châteaux familiar from travel posters and brochures. Sadly, many visitors see only the famous sites, dashing from Amboise to Chambord and from Cheverny to Villandry. What they are missing is a tapestry rich with the threads of history, involving the ambitious English and the artistic Italians, influential authors such as Pierre de Ronsard and François Rabelais, centres of learning in Saumur and Angers and ancient abbeys such as Fontevraud, all bound together by a major highway – La Loire.

The stretch of the Loire known as the Val de Loire, from Gien to Angers, is lined with towns, such as Blois, that offer more than just a castle; similarly, Beaugency and Meung-sur-Loire have more to see than many villages.

As for cities, Orléans has memories of Joan of Arc, while Tours blends a large student population with 1,700 years of history. Further south is Bourges, too little visited but boasting a

magnificent cathedral and old quarter.

The valley also encompasses the tributaries of the Loire, each with its own châteaux: Chenonceau on the Cher, Le Lude on the Loir, Chinon on the Vienne, Azay-le-Rideau on the Indre. There are also small châteaux, still lived in by their owners, where the elegantly furnished *salons* are as much 'home' as 'museum'.

Over the last decade the region has seen extensive restoration work as well as

THE LOIRE VALLEY

High and mighty: Saumur's castle has dominated the landscape for five centuries

an astonishing growth in attractions and museums, though the popular *son et lumière* (sound and light) shows still bring silent stone battlements to life on summer evenings, often with a cast of hundreds, plus horses and fireworks.

And then there is the wine: still, *pétillant* and sparkling; red, white and *rosé*; dry, medium and sweet. No wonder this is a region that demands time ... in a most polite way, of course, since according to proud locals, this is where the 'best' French is spoken.

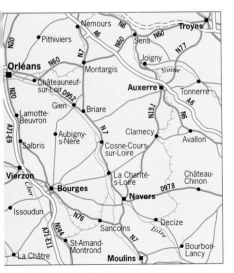

LOCATOR

History

52BC–5th century AD

Julius Caesar conquers Touraine and other parts of the Celtic provinces of Gaul. The Loire Valley comes within the Roman province of *Lugdunensis*. Caesar is believed to have crossed the river east of Orléans, at St-Benoît-sur-Loire. The Gallo-Roman period continues until the barbarian invasions of the 4th century bring an end to Roman rule.

AD250

St Gatien is sent from Rome to convert Gaul to Christianity, becoming the first bishop of Tours.

451

The Huns, led by Attila, beseige Orléans, but are driven off by the townspeople, led by their bishop, St Aignan, aided by a timely storm. The Huns leave Gaul.

732

Another invasion is repulsed when Charles Martel defeats the Moors (Saracens) at Poitiers (some believe the battle took place near Ste-Maure).

11th century

The region's first major stone fortifications are constructed by Foulques III Nerra (see page 71), the ambitious Count of Anjou (the Tour Carrée in Loudun and the keeps at Loches and Langeais are still visible today).

1154

Henri Plantagenet, Count of Anjou, is crowned King Henry II of England.

1189

The death of Henry II, at Chinon, marks the start of a 300-year struggle between the kings of England and France for supremacy in the Loire Valley.

1199

King Richard the Lionheart dies at Châlus and is buried, like his father, Henry II, at Fontevraud.

1337

The Hundred Years' War begins as King Edward III of England pushes his claim to French territory.

1417

King Henry V of England fights his way to Bourges. Three years later, the Treaty of Troyes recognises him as heir to the throne of France and gives him King Charles VI's daughter, Catherine, in marriage.

KING HENRY THE II

1429

Jeanne d'Arc (Joan of Arc) joins forces with the Dauphin (the uncrowned King Charles VII of France) and defeats the English at Orléans. French spirits are revived with Charles VII's coronation at Reims. Even so, the Hundred Years' War rumbles on until the English are finally defeated at Castillon in 1453.

1460–1600
The flowering of the 'Royal Valley of the Loire'. Successive kings build magnificent châteaux and courtly life flourishes. In 1494, after his military adventures in Italy, King Charles VIII returns to France influenced by Italian culture. He rebuilds the château at Amboise in the new, grandiose Renaissance style.

Maid of Orléans: the pedestal of Jeanne d'Arc's statue in the city she rescued

1519
Great artists and writers flourish in the region. Leonardo da Vinci dies at Amboise. The construction of Chambord is underway.

1562–98
The Wars of Religion (see pages 58–9). Persecuted Huguenots (Protestants) retaliate by looting Catholic abbeys and churches. In 1588 the leader of the Catholic faction, the powerful Duc de Guise, is murdered at Blois by supporters of the Huguenot King Henri III. A year later, the king is assassinated and succeeded by the Huguenot Henri IV of Navarre. He crushes the Catholics but then converts to Catholicism, unifying the country and ending the wars. His Edict of Nantes (1598) guarantees freedom of worship to the Huguenots. The court moves back to Paris; the years of the 'Royal Valley of the Loire' are over.

1789
The French Revolution begins, followed four years later by the Vendée Wars in which royalists revolt against the republicans. Cholet, Fontenay and Saumur fall to the royalist rebels before they are massacred by the government's

colonnes infernales ('Troops from Hell'). The war kills half the population of the Vendée.

1832
The first steamboat chugs down the River Loire, but the railways soon take over, marking the river's decline as a transport link.

1870
The Prussians capture Châteaudun, Orléans, Tours and Azay-le-Rideau during the month-long Franco-Prussian War.

1940
During World War II, France's aged Marshal Pétain shakes hands with Hitler at Montoire-sur-le-Loire, a symbol of collaboration with the enemy. The Cher river marks the division between Occupied and 'Vichy' France.

1969
France's first and controversial atomic power station opens at Avoine, near Chinon, on the Loire.

1989
The TGV high-speed train links the Loire Valley to Paris.

Geography and Economy

*T*he great expanse of the Loire Valley encompasses several age-old provinces that were once important names in French history: Orléanais, the largest; Touraine, known for its wealth; and Anjou, the land of the Plantagenets. Now this area is divided between the Pays de la Loire and the Centre-Val-de-Loire. Both are modern bureaucratic inventions that embrace half-a-dozen *départements*.

The Pays de la Loire

Enveloping the western end of the Loire Valley, the Pays de la Loire has some three million inhabitants scattered over 32,500sq km. Nantes, the administrative capital, and Angers together account for some 700,000 of the population, the rest being spread around the towns and villages of the wide-open countryside. About one in 10 is employed in agriculture, where there has been a dramatic drop of 50 per cent in employment in the past 15 years,

Don't be confused: Le Loir is a pretty tributary of the bigger Loire

emphasising a rise in efficiency rarely recognised outside France. This is one of France's principal livestock rearing regions, but the processing of fresh produce is just as important. Canning companies, such as Fleury Michon and Saupiquet, dairies such as Bel and Yoplait, and biscuit and cake manufacturers, such as St-Michel, BN and LU, all make a substantial contribution to the local economy. In Angers, the humble orange is transformed into Cointreau liqueur.

Nantes has France's second largest *bourse* (stock exchange) while the thriving leather and shoe industry has

Limestone gives Saumur its nickname of *La Ville Blanche*, the white town

long been a Vendée speciality. Overall, 25 per cent of the workforce is involved in manufacturing, especially in the rapidly rising field of electronics and electrical goods.

TRIBUTARIES OF THE LOIRE

The Loire is famous for its noble châteaux; though many of the finest are not on the Loire itself; tributaries such as the Cher, Indre, Vienne, and Layon (flowing into the Loire from the south), and the Cisse, Loir, Sarthe, Mayenne and Oudon (entering from the north) all have their own attractive châteaux set in landscapes of great variety.

Centre-Val-de-Loire

This area, combining Touraine and Berry, with Orléans as the administrative capital, includes large tracts of forest and the semi-wilderness of the Sologne. It is even more sparsely populated than the Pays de la Loire, with fewer than 2.5 million inhabitants, spread over 40,000sq km, an average of 62.5 inhabitants per sq km. Here, too, farming claims 10 per cent of the workforce in an area that ranks as the fourth biggest in agricultural production in France, while in the region north of Orléans, the Beauce ranks number one for cereals. The Poulain chocolate factories at Blois are significant local employers, along with the automotive industry: Matra cars at Romorantin, SNIAS at Bourges and Michelin at Joué-les-Tours. The region's combined electronic, chemical and pharmaceutical production ranks second only to the Ile de France in the whole country.

Tourism

Tourism is important to the Loire Valley economy, but the people here have recognised that being the land of famous châteaux is not enough. In every city and town, scaffolding signifies that work is in progress to restore medieval and Renaissance buildings. Great effort is put into cultural events and regional festivals. The quality of life in the Loire valley has been celebrated for centuries; locals are working hard to keep it that way.

THE LOIRE

The Loire is the longest river in France. It bubbles up at Gerbier-de-Jonc only 150km from the Mediterranean. It then flows north for much of its course, before sweeping westwards at Sancerre towards the Atlantic. The statistics are impressive: the Loire is over 1,000km long, with a 1,400m drop in altitude from the source high in the Cévennes mountains to the 3km-wide mouth at St-Nazaire on the Atlantic Coast. On the way, the river cuts through eleven *départements* and drains water from one fifth of the whole land area of France.

For centuries the Loire was a major transport route, carrying goods and people. Timber, fruit and wine would be loaded aboard flat-bottomed *chalands* and *gabarres*, boats that could slide on and off the notorious shoals and sand banks without damage. Fish from the Atlantic would be kept alive in tanks of salt water and rowed slowly upstream against the current. Only in the 19th century did the coming of the railway diminish its importance.

Today, roads follow built-up embankments, often looking down to the river on one side and to the roofs of houses on the other. Broad and flat, the Loire may appear docile, but it is a dangerous river. Some *turcies* (earthen ramparts) were built 1,000 years ago in an early attempt to control the floods. Further defences were built along the Authion tributary in the 12th century; *levées* (raised banks) were built by Colbert, the finance minister of King Louis XIV, in the 17th century. Still the floods ripped through, causing disasters in 1846, 1856 and 1866. Early in 1995, the banks once again barely contained the inundation.

Flooding is not the only danger. Between the river's islands are the treacherous *sables mouvants* (quicksands) ready to suck in the unwary picnicker or walker. *Tourbillons* (whirlpools) do the same to kayaks and canoes exploring the apparently innocuous *boires* (side channels) or *luisettes* (rivulets).

Left: early
morning at
Briare-le-Canal

Below: up a lazy
river. Sand banks
abound, even in
the heart of
Orléans

Modern developments
have also made their mark.
Atomic power stations
occasionally scar the
landscape and, since 1989,
the TGV high-speed train
has brought Paris within
commuting distance.

Despite this, nature
remains in charge of the
Loire. Stately herons and flickering
kingfishers, catfish and *sandre* (zander)
all abound, and even the salmon are
making an enthusiastic come-back.

Everywhere the land seems fertile. No
wonder it attracted the nobility of France
and was called the Vallée des Rois, the
Valley of the Kings.

Regions of the Loire

*I*f there is one physical feature that unites the 450km of the valley of the Loire, from Nantes to Nevers, it has to be overall flatness. There are no granite outcrops or towering escarpments, no ranges of high hills or cavernous gorges. There are, however, gentle undulations where the Loire and its side rivers have cut through the ubiquitous limestone to produce cliffs, often topped by a castle.

A well-lit landscape

Sweeping horizons and vast skyscapes flood the region with light: châteaux are silhouetted against blue skies, vineyards and wheatfields are drenched with sunshine and even small clumps of trees look prettier in the region's clear light. North and south of Angers, away from the Loire, are patchworks of small, hedged fields and farms; the slopes running down to the river itself are covered in vines. East of Angers, where the River Authion runs almost parallel to the Loire, the fertile soil is worked by market gardeners and nurserymen.

Limestone and forest

The region's chalky white rock has been quarried for centuries to build palaces and mansions, castles and abbeys. The resulting holes in the cliffs have been used as homes (*caves troglodites*) by ordinary folk. The once-abundant forests have been chopped down to build the scores of medieval houses that still survive in almost all the region's towns

Rural peace near Bourges

Hidden treasure: Montsoreau's wine is stored deep in the cliffs

and cities. On the southern side of the Loire, around Saumur, low cliffs of *tuffe* (tufa) are riddled with ancient caves and tunnels, now recycled for use as wine storage cellars and mushroom farms.

Fertile fields

Further south in the Saumur region are vines. In the north around Baugé, the ancient forest has now dwindled to scattered areas of woodland, interspersed with fields of sunflowers and maize. Between Saumur and Tours, the broad valley is filled with orchards and vegetable growers. To the south is Ste-Maure, the plateau which gives its name to the famous goat's cheese. North of Tours is the Gâtine; now drained and cultivated, the area consists of a mixture of fields, woodland and open heath.

Dense forests, misty marshes and vines

South of Orléans is the region known as the Sologne. The thick forests near Orléans are slowly being invaded by golf courses. This traditional land of misty, murky marshes has also been changed by the extraction of clay for brick making, leaving behind a series of ponds. Now rather scrubby, this is the flattest part of the region, covered in small pines and heather and still known for its hunting. North of Orléans are the plains of the Beauce, for centuries the breadbasket of France with its endless fields of wheat. Finally, to the south of Gien, the corrugated slopes along the Loire are embroidered with vines; these grow the Sauvignon Blanc grapes that produce the famous Sancerre and Pouilly wines.

Politics

*P*olitically, the Loire Valley is a conservative area, where change is rarely welcomed. Tours, for example, has had a right-wing mayor for 35 years who, although popular for his conservation projects, is nevertheless criticised for the lack of investment in industry. In local elections, voters support the individual, rather than a party. Communist mayors are not uncommon, even in the 1990s, and Orléans, traditionally right-wing, moved left at the last elections. French politics are unpredictable.

Political parties

France has five recognisable political parties. The RPR (Rassemblement pour la République) sprang from the old Gaullist party of General de Gaulle. The RPR is business-orientated and

Liberté, Egalité, Fraternité: the Town Hall is the heart of French politics

encourages privatisation, and low taxation. The UDF (Union pour la Démocratie Française) is a right-of-centre party that tends to work in coalition with the RPR. The PS (Parti Socialiste) has moved towards the centre (pro-Europe and pro-NATO) while the PCF (Parti Communiste Français) has slumped in popularity since World War II. The party that has received most publicity in recent years is the FN (Front National), the ultra-right-wing party led by Jean-Marie le Pen.

Administration

In the 1980s, France's highly centralised government structure was reorganised; in theory, power was devolved to the grassroots. Justice, education and health remain national responsibilities. In the next layer down, France is divided into 22 regions, of which the Pays de la Loire (Western Loire) and Centre-Val-de-Loire are two. The regions administer tourism, cultural heritage, industrial development and adult education. Below the regional level are France's 96 *départements*, which oversee social services and welfare. Finally, the *départements* are further subdivided into 36,500 *communes*, each headed by a mayor who is often a powerful political figure, responsible for local planning, building and environmental controls.

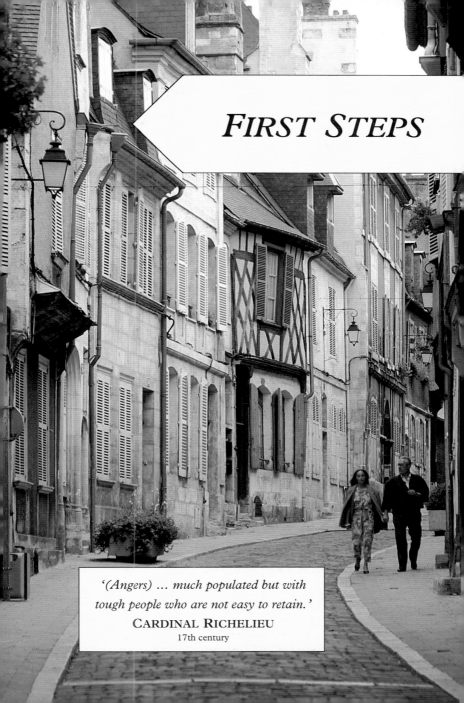

FIRST STEPS

'(Angers) ... much populated but with
tough people who are not easy to retain.'
CARDINAL RICHELIEU
17th century

First Steps

THE PEOPLE

The people of the Loire are totally French in outlook and manners, and they have no distinctive character traits or looks. Neither do they have a peasant folklore, colourful costumes, music or dances. What they have long had, however, is, according to 19th-century novelist, Honoré de Balzac, 'a refined spirit, a politeness that befits a region that the kings of France have taken to their hearts.' Even today, the inhabitants of the Loire are still 'completely relaxed, because they have so little character', according to contemporary novelist Jean-Marie Laclavetine. His view that this welcoming relaxed attitude is due to a lack of character, is not a criticism; rather he is complimenting people for their moderation and lack of confrontation.

Their equable nature reflects the environment, which has neither extremes of climate nor of landscape. The ingredients of the good life are readily to hand, from field, stream and vineyard. No wonder locals boast of their *art de bien vivre*, an 'art of living well' that includes not just a love of fine food and wine, but also a developed culture that dates back to the French Renaissance which, after all, had its

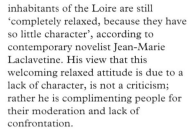

Left: the people of the Loire
Below: it's better by bike

origins in the Loire 500 years ago. All this is good news for international visitors. From hoteliers to campsite managers and from guides to winegrowers, everyone is used to dealing with tourists and understands the different tastes of different nationalities. There is a welcome informality throughout the region, so 'smart-casual' clothing is acceptable almost everywhere, except in churches and cathedrals where shorts and sleeveless tops are seen as offensive. The custom of muttering 'M'sieurs, dames' on entering a shop or restaurant prevails, as does the handshake with new acquaintances.

With English now the region's second language, it is easy to strike up conversations – but do take advice with a pinch of salt. The local wine and the local château will always be recommended because, despite their worldliness, the people of the Loire believe that their home town or village is the best place on earth.

GETTING ABOUT

The Loire Valley has a mixture of main roads for fast intercity traffic and delightfully rural lanes for gentle sightseeing. More motorways are being built, linking Le Mans to Angers and Nantes, while Orléans is already connected to Tours and Bourges. Although the main riverside roads can be very busy – sometimes limited to only one lane in each direction on a high dike or embankment – there is usually a quiet, if meandering, riverside road on the opposite bank of the Loire. Since the countryside is generally flat or gently undulating, this is especially good cycling country, and a large-scale map makes it easy for cyclists to follow the well-paved minor roads.

THOMAS COOK'S LOIRE VALLEY

As early as 1890, Thos Cook et Fils ran excursions from Paris to the Loire and the Vendée. A 30-day package cost a mere 155FF – and that was first class! British visitors were encouraged to enjoy 'the most delicious of climates, the most romantic of rivers, the most idyllic of scenery, the most wonderful of chateaux'. Then, as now, 'catering seems to be an easy and pleasurable occupation.'

OPENING HOURS

There is a bewildering variety of opening hours but, in general, all sights are open daily in July and August.

Museums tend to open from 10am to 6pm, with two hours for lunch; most close for all, or part, of Monday or Tuesday.

Ruined castles and abbeys are open during daylight hours – usually until 7pm in summer, but closing at 4pm in winter. Most are closed on national holidays. At many châteaux, you are not allowed to wander at will; instead you must join what can be a lengthy guided tour of an hour or more.

Churches are normally open from 8am to noon, and from 2pm to 7pm or later, but you are discouraged from visiting during services.

Do phone ahead when planning a specific outing, particularly if you want to join a guided tour.

CHÂTEAUX OF THE LOIRE

Chenonceau and Azay-le-Rideau, mirrored in water; Ussé, with its fairy-tale towers; Chambord, the grandiose royal hunting lodge; and Cheverny, the country mansion – these are the architectural descendants of the simple wood and earth forts of northern France, originally built in the 8th and 9th centuries as protection against quarrelsome neighbours as well as Viking and Muslim raiders. Their evolution can be traced over 800 years.

8th–11th centuries

First came the motte-and-bailey construction. The motte was an earthen mound defended by a deep ditch. At the base of the mound, the 'bailey' was a stockade enclosing farm buildings and storehouses. On top of the mound, another stockade defended a fort, as in the reconstruction in the Parc de la Haie-Joulain at St-Sylvain d'Anjou near Angers. Timber forts were later rebuilt in stone, resulting in the *donjon* (a keep, not a dungeon). Foulques III Nerra (see page 71) built many such *donjons*, the remains of which can be seen at Langeais (see page 68), Loches (see page 70) and Beaugency (see page 92).

12th–13th centuries
Military architects, learning from the lessons of the Crusades, built curtain walls to protect the buildings of the inner keep, with circular lookout towers at intervals around the walls. Narrow slits allowed archers to fire outwards, and machicolations (holes in the floor) were used for dropping stones and quicklime, but not boiling oil, on attackers. At Angers (see page 26) and Chinon (see page 64), the impressive walls, their smoothness an added protection, encompassed extensive living quarters and chapels.

14th–15th centuries
Once the Hundred Years' War with England was over in 1453, defence gave way to grandeur. At Langeais, built between 1465 and 1469, turreted towers are softened by domestic-looking gables and larger windows. Older castles were remodelled and given fine interiors. Moats became mirrors and water gardens rather than defences. By the late 15th century, several châteaux were being renovated as royal palaces. At Amboise (see page 60), King Charles VIII surrounded himself with luxurious furnishings copied from the palaces of Italy.

16th century
King Louis XII (1498–1515) established his court at Blois (see page 94). His successor, King François I enlarged Amboise and built Chambord (see page 94), while his Secretary of State created Villandry (see page 79) with its

magnificent gardens. Chenonceau (see page 62) was made grand first by the mistress of King Henri II, Diane de Poitiers, and then by his widow, Catherine de'Medici. The end of the royal era in the Loire came in 1598 when King Henri IV, the first of the Bourbons, moved the court back to Paris.

17th–18th centuries
Even without the king, the Loire continued to attract the wealthy and the aristocratic. Cheverny was built (see page 98), and at Saumur (see page 42) and Chaumont (see page 62) walls were removed to open up the vistas. Violence returned, however, when many châteaux were stripped bare or destroyed during the French Revolution (1789–92).

Royal presence: King Louis XII was born and held court in Blois

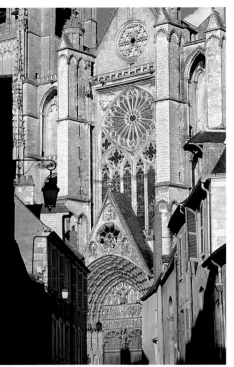
Medieval marvel: Bourges has one of France's finest cathedrals

THE MAIN SIGHTS

Châteaux

The châteaux of the Loire come in all shapes and sizes, from menacing medieval fortresses to romantic mansions, and from royal palaces to glorified country retreats. There are hundreds and it is all too easy to cram too many into an itinerary. As one tourist officer admitted, 'one château a day is enough, two is hard work and three is ridiculous.' Prevent an overdose of castles by looking at the outside of many but going inside just a few.

To help you choose which to visit, bear in mind that some of the state-owned buildings are virtually empty, except for a few pieces of furniture and the inevitable faded tapestries. Privately owned châteaux have to work harder to attract tourists, and many provide more for the entrance fee. Those that are still lived in have a refreshing family ambience.

Classic cathedrals, awesome abbeys

Churches and abbeys such as Solesmes, Cunault and St-Benoît-sur-Loire echo to the voices of monks who still sing in Gregorian chant. Fontevraud, resting place of English kings, is used for classical recordings because the acoustics are so good. The simplicity of these abbey churches contrasts with the complex decoration of Bourges cathedral, with its stunning stained glass. Smaller gems are also to be found: the stained glass at the Ste-Chapelle in Champigny-sur-Veude, near Richelieu; and the startling mosaic ceiling in the tiny chapel of St-Germigny-des-Prés (perhaps France's oldest church) are among the best.

Sophisticated towns and cities

With its exciting mixture of half-timbered medieval and decorated Renaissance houses, plus an international student body, Tours vibrates like no other city in the area. Angers, too, benefits from having a university to enliven its atmosphere and add to the cultural life. Bourges is a gem often overlooked by foreigners, while Orléans is an important business city. Blois has a large pedestrian area full of tempting shops while Amboise, Chinon and Loches all have delightful old streets beneath their châteaux. Saumur is a must, particularly for anyone interested in wine and horses.

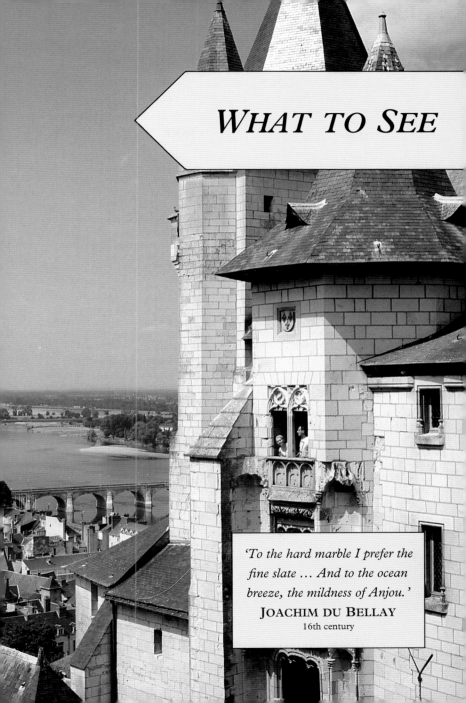

WHAT TO SEE

'To the hard marble I prefer the fine slate ... And to the ocean breeze, the mildness of Anjou.'

JOACHIM DU BELLAY
16th century

The Western Loire

*T*he city of Nantes (once the capital of Brittany) sits at the westernmost end of the Val de Loire. To the east is Saumur, known as '*la ville blanche*' (the white town) because of the soft white tufa limestone quarried near by. In between these two cities is Angers, historic capital of the Counts of Anjou, known as '*la ville noire*' (the black town) because of its nearby slate mines. The centuries old rivalry dates back to the 16th century when Angers was a Catholic stronghold, Saumur a powerful Protestant enclave.

North of Angers, the rolling countryside is veined by rivers, many dotted by *péniches* (houseboats) that drift peacefully past sleepy villages. Near by, privately owned châteaux – such as Montgeoffroy and Serrant, le Plessis-Macé and le Plessis-Bourré – echo with long-forgotten intrigue, the moat and drawbridge now a last line of defence against tourists shooting with long lens cameras.

To the northeast of Angers, in the Loir valley (a tributary of the bigger Loire), are La Flèche, home of France's

Angers: the art deco Maison Bleue on boulevard Maréchal Foch

prestigious military academy, and Le Lude, enlivened each summer by a historical drama of light and fireworks put on by local townspeople.

North of the Loire, the houses and castles are roofed in grey-blue slate, mined at Trélazé. South of the Loire, red clay roof tiles hint at the architecture of the Mediterranean. To the west, an endless sea of vines produces Muscadet, sharp as a green apple. To the east, round Saumur, red wines and sparkling *vins mousseux* are tended in cool dark caverns that are also a temporary home to millions of mushrooms. Other caves are hidden beneath the plains round Doué-la-Fontaine, the City of Roses, to

THE WESTERN LOIRE

Châteaubourg • Vitré • Montsûrs • Evron • Sillé-le-Guillaume • Conlie • Ballon
RENNES N157 *Vilaine* • Argentré • Ste-Suzanne • D194
Châteaugiron • A81 E50 • A81 E50 • A81 E50 • N138
Janzé • NI57 • Laval • Bazougers • D21 • St-Denis-d'Orques • N157
La Guerche-de-Bretagne • Meslay-du-Maine • Brûlon • Loué • LE MANS
Retiers • Vaignes • A11 • Arnage
Bain-de-Bretagne • Martigné-Ferchaud • Laubrières • Cossé-le-Vivien • Grez-en-Bouère • Abb de Solesmes • La Suze-sur-Sarthe • N138
Rougé • St-Aignan-sur-Roe • Craon • Château-Gontier • Sablé-sur-Sarthe • Malicorne-sur-Sarthe • Ecommoy
NI71 • Miré • Sarthe
Châteaubriant • Pouancé • Segré • Châteauneuf-sur-Sarthe • La Flèche • Pontvallain Mayet
Derval • Combrée • D306 • Durtal • Parc Zool du Tertre Rouge
St-Julien-de-Vouvantes • La Chapelle-Glain • Chât de la Loire • Le Lion d'Angers • Champigné • Tiercé • Seiches-sur-Loir • D766 • Le Lude • D959
Nozay • Don • Riaillé • Chât de l'Isle-Briand • Chât du Plessis-Bourré • Chât de Baugé • Forêt de Chandelais
Grand Réservoir de Voireau • Erdre • St-Mars-la-Jaille • Château du Plessis-Macé • Genneteil
Candé • Bécon-les-Granits • ANGERS • Montgeoffroy • Noyant
Nort-sur-Erdre • E60 A11 • St-Georges • Les Ponts-de-Cé • Trélazé • Beaufort-en-Vallée • Linières-Rillé • Bouton
Ancenis • Varades • sur-Loire • Chât de Serrant • Mazé • Longué-Jumelles • Gizeux
Carquefou • Champtoceaux • Liré • Chalonnes • Brissac-Quincé • Les Rosiers • Vernantes
Château de la Bourgonnière • St-Florent-le-Vieil • Corniche Angevine • Chât de Boumois • Allonnes • Bourgueil
NANTES • Thouaré-sur-Loire • St-Laurent-de-la-Plaine • St-Lambert-du-Lattay • Chât de Brissac • Cunault • Saumur • Chât d'Ussé
Château de Goulaine • Le Loroux-Bottereau • Martigné • Thouarcé • Doué-la-Fontaine • Montsoreau • Chinon
St-Phibert-de-Grand Lieu • Vallet • St-Macaire-en-Mauges • Chemillé • Vihiers • Parc Zool des Minières • Montreuil-Bellay • Fontevraud-l'Abbaye
Aigrefeuille-sur-Maine • Clisson • Le Puy-N-D • Chât • Richelieu
Montaigu • Mortagne-sur-Sèvre • Maulévrier • Argenton-Château • Les Trois-Moutiers • Loudun
Rocheservière • Les Herbiers • St-Laurent-sur-Sèvre • Les Aubiers • Thouars • Monts-sur-Guesnes
Legé • Le Puy-du-Fou • Mauléon • St-Jouin-de-Marnes • Lencloître
St-Fulgent • St-Michel Mt-Mercure • Bressuire • Airvault • Mirebeau
Belleville-sur-Vie • Cerizay
Le Poiré-sur-Vie • Les Essarts • Pouzauges • 0 10 20 30 40 50 km

the west of which the film actor, Gérard Depardieu, has a vineyard. These secret attractions are matched by the little-known dessert wines of the Coteaux du Layon and the village of Clisson, an Italian style *città* deep in the French countryside, complete with its *campanile* (belltower).

The war that raged here two centuries ago, between local royalists and republicans is commemorated with monuments and the red handkerchiefs sold in souvenir shops. Living history is encapsulated at the abbeys of Solesmes and Cunault where the monks chant services in timeless plainsong. In Baugé, a small chapel is home to the famous double cross, symbol of Anjou, then of Lorraine, and then of the Free France movement in World War II.

Angers

*A*ngers straddles a river – not the Loire, the longest in France, but the Maine, the shortest. Formed by the confluence of the Loir, Mayenne and Sarthe, it flows for only 5km before emptying into the Loire, southwest of the city. Centuries ago, Angers was an important port, with ships sailing up from the Atlantic. Today, the important link is with Paris: by TGV the French capital is only 1½ hours away from this bustling city of 220,000, with two universities and a thriving city centre.

The city dates back to a Roman settlement, founded in 14BC as the capital of the region ruled by the Celtic Andes tribe. As the old capital of Anjou, it was the power base for leaders such as Foulques III Nerra (see page 71) who, in the 11th century, built churches, a stone bridge over the river and a new settlement, La Doutre, on the western

Garden centre: flowers now soften the ramparts of Angers castle

bank. The castle was built as a defence against the English, whose claim to French lands stemmed from the crowning of Henri, Count of Anjou, as King Henry II of England. Later wars left their mark. The Wars of Religion saw a massacre of local Protestants in 1572. Over two centuries later, in the Revolutionary period, fighting erupted again, this time between republicans and royalists, based in the nearby Vendée region to the southwest.

The art of the loom: Angers' 600-year-old Apocalypse Tapestries

Not all of Angers' history is military. Its reputation for culture dates back to the 15th century and the best-loved Angevin of all: le Bon Roi René (see box). Today, the city is a centre of weaving, home to the medieval Apocalypse Tapestries and the modern *Chant du Monde*, as well as the Regional Centre for Textile Art. Although the bridges, law courts, gardens and theatre date mainly from 19th century, the old quarter by the imposing fortress boasts photogenic medieval and Renaissance buildings, some now housing museums. On the outskirts are well-kept suburbs and modern *zones industrielles*, where computer and electronics companies are located, as well as the distillery that produces the famous orange liqueur, Cointreau, a 150-year-old local business.

LE BON ROI RENÉ (1409–1480)

Good King René was never the king of France and he was only king of Hungary, Jerusalem, and Naples in name. He was, however, Count of Anjou. Educated and enlightened, he loved music, literature and gardens and bequeathed the Apocalypse Tapestries to the cathedral. His huge festivals, inspired by the age of chivalry, were immensely popular. His youthful statue stands in the middle of the traffic near Angers château where he was born. He died in Provence, after Anjou had been annexed by the French under King Louis XI.

Rose window: medieval stained glass in Angers' cathedral

Cathédrale St-Maurice

Standing high above the river, this compact 12th-century cathedral has no flying buttresses and no side aisles. Either side of the door are figures from the Old Testament (note the long plaits and slim waist of Esther) whilst higher up the façade are statues representing St Maurice and his companions. Inside, the nave is typical of the 'Angevin Gothic' or 'Plantagenet' style. The chancel is the burial place of the Counts of Anjou, including Good King René. The 12th- to 16th-century stained-glass windows are the glory of the cathedral. The chancel window 15th from the left depicts the Martyrdom of St Thomas à Becket which took place in 1170 and so was a fairly recent event when the glass was made.
Place Freppel.

Le Château

Forget the Renaissance extravagance of châteaux elsewhere in the Loire Valley: this 13th-century fortress impresses by its sheer mass. Made of alternating bands of shale and tufa, the horizontal white and black lines emphasise the 1km-length of the perimeter wall, guarded by 17 towers. Now standing between 40 and 50m in height, they were even more dominating before the tops were dismantled during the Wars of Religion. Constructed between 1230 and 1239, the castle replaced a wooden fort built by Foulques III Nerra, who is supposed to have thrown his wife from the ramparts after discovering her infidelity. Today, the peaceful ramparts support a herb garden and vines.

A specially built gallery houses La Tenture de L'Apocalypse (The Apocalypse Tapestry), the world's largest tapestry based on an illustrated manuscript of the *Book of the Apocalypse*. Woven between 1373 and 1383, it is 130m long and 4.5m high. Although the symbolism may be confusing, the overall theme is the battle between good and evil. Each of the six 'chapters' tells a story, introduced by a narrator. Gruesome scenes of death and destruction are enlightened by humorous border details, such as the rabbit diving into its burrow below panel 37 and popping out again on panel 51.

Originally, only a few panels were shown at a time, though the whole was taken to Arles and displayed for the wedding of Louis I of Anjou, father of Good King René. During the Revolution, it was cut up and discarded; fortunately, most of the pieces were discovered and reassembled in 1848. You can appreciate the tapestries on many levels: by following the story with

Bible in hand, by admiring the technical skill needed for weaving a butterfly or a horse's mane, or simply by looking at the faces whose emotions are recognisable and vivid even after 600 years. To understand the history and symbolism fully, join a tour or rent the headphones. Of the original 90 tapestries, 75 still remain.
Tel: 41 87 43 47. Open: daily. Closed: public holidays. Admission charge.

La Distillerie Cointreau (Cointreau Distillery)

Sniff the dried orange peel which flavours this famous liqueur. The 1-hour guided tour shows the distilling process but the recipe remains secret.
Espace Cointreau, Carrefour Molière, St-Barthélémy. Tel: 41 43 25 21. Open: mid-June to mid-September, tours at 10am, 11am, 2pm, 3pm, 4pm weekdays, 3pm and 4.30pm weekends and public holidays; rest of year, 3pm and 4.30pm on Sunday and public holidays only. Closed: 23 December to 2 January and 1 May. Admission charge.

Galerie David d'Angers

A ruined medieval abbey with a modern roof is the dramatic setting for plaster casts donated by the famous romantic sculptor, Pierre-Jean David (1788–1856), known as David d'Angers, after his birth place. The casts are from statues of famous men, such as Voltaire, Gutenberg, Goethe and Balzac.
33–37 bis, rue Toussaint. Tel: 41 87 21 03. Open: daily. Closed: Mondays and public holidays. Admission charge.

Maison d'Adam

Adam and Eve were removed in the French Revolution, but this half-timbered merchant's house, built around 1500, still has its carved Annunciation scene, a pelican feeding three chicks and a man with three testicles. Now it is a shop selling local crafts, including tapestries.
Corner of rue Montault and place Ste-Croix.

Left: the Maison d'Adam
Below: gardens have replaced the water in the moat of Angers' castle

Le Chant du Monde tapestry

Musée des Beaux-Arts
(Le Logis Barrault)

This better-than-average provincial art gallery has 18th-century French-school paintings and sculptures by Fragonard, Watteau, Ingres and Corot, housed in the handsome late 15th-century Logis Barrault. The Comice pear was developed by the local horticultural association in the gardens in 1849.
10 rue du Musée. Tel: 41 88 64 65. Open: see Galerie David d'Angers. Admission charge.

Musée Jean Lurçat et de la Tapisserie Contemporaine

Jean Lurçat, an Aubusson weaver, was inspired by the Apocalypse Tapestry to design the vibrant *Le Chant du Monde* (the Song of the World) between 1957 and 1966. It hangs in the 12th-century Hôpital St-Jean, in the La Doutre suburb, next door to which is the CRAT Regional Centre for Textile Art, where visitors can watch weavers at work.
Museum: 4 boulevard Arago. Tel: 41 87 41 06. Open: see Galerie David d'Angers. Admission charge.
Centre Régionale: 3 boulevard Davier. Tel: 41 87 10 88. Open: weekdays. Free.

ANCENIS

Once an important port for shipping wine, the town is dominated by the 500m-long suspension bridge over the Loire. The arms of Brittany and Anjou at opposite ends recall the ancient boundary. Little more than the twin turrets and the Renaissance Grand Logis (hall) remain of the castle.

Liré

Two kilometres south of Ancenis, a dusty museum honours 16th-century poet Joachim du Bellay, born here in 1522.
Tel: 40 09 04 13. Open: daily, closed Monday and Friday; July and August, closed Monday. Admission charge.

Ancenis is 45km west of Angers on the north bank of the Loire.

BAUGÉ

The treasure here is not the 15th-century château but a medieval crucifix studded with gold and gems. *La Vraie Croix* is made from a piece of the 'true cross' of Christ, which was brought back from the Holy Land in 1241. The two crosspieces are a distinctive feature of the cross of Anjou. In 1940, General de Gaulle made it the symbol of Free France.
Chapelle des Filles de Coeur de Marie, 8 rue de la Girouardière. Tel: 41 89 12 20. Open: afternoons, Wednesday to Monday. Donation requested.

L'Apothicairerie

Upstairs in the local hospital is a fascinating pharmacy of 1650, full of blue glass bottles and decorated *chevrettes* (porcelain jars).
L'Hôpital de Baugé. Tel: 41 89 18 07. Open: daily. Admission charge.

THE VENDÉE WARS

Not everyone saw the French Revolution as a liberating force. Southwest of Angers, the people of the Vendée region took up arms in support of the king. The blood-red handkerchiefs made in Cholet were worn as a badge of courage by *les Blancs* (the Whites, or royalists) and windmill sails were used to send messages: an X signalled 'calm', but an upright cross meant 'assemble'.

This bloody war produced its heroes. Napoleon Bonaparte, a general of *les Bleus* (the Blue, or republican army) called the Vendée the 'land of the giants' after 3,000 peasants held off his army of 25,000. The royalist General Bonchamps, defeated and mortally wounded at Cholet, begged his men not to massacre 5,000 captured republicans, held at St-Florent-le-Vieil, in revenge.

Two centuries on, reminders of the wars remain. The symbol of the Vendée – two hearts under a cross and crown – stands for loyalty to God and king. Some villages still resolutely ignore the Bastille Day celebrations of 14 July.

Baugé is 40km east of Angers on the D766.

BOUMOIS, CHÂTEAU DE

This lovely 16th-century château was the birthplace of Captain Aristide Dupetit-Thouars (1760–98). Horribly mutilated at the Battle of the Nile in 1798, he ordered his sailors to put his bleeding torso into a barrel of bran on the quarter-deck of his ship, the *Tonnant*, so that he could carry on with the battle, with no thought of surrender. The château contains mementoes of the Dupetit-Thouars family, and a fine full-length portrait of Queen Elizabeth I of England. *45km southeast of Angers on the north bank of the Loire, near St-Martin-de-la-Place. Tel: 41 38 43 16. Open: daily, July and August Wednesday to Monday, Palm Sunday to 30 June and September to November. Admission charge.*

Rich mixture: Boumois architecture is part-Gothic, part-Renaissance

Tall story: the Château de Brissac towers a full seven storeys high

BRISSAC, CHÂTEAU DE

'*Si je n'étais dauphin, je voudrais être Brissac,*' sighed the future King Henri II in 1542 ('If I weren't heir to the throne, I'd like to be a Brissac.'). The Dukes of Brissac still call this home – all 204 rooms of it. Set on the Aubance river, two chunks of the original 15th-century castle guard the densely decorated *pavillon* (central façade). The interior is fascinating and features a red and gold theatre built for an ancestor with a fine voice, and a portrait of the famous Veuve (Widow) Clicquot who gave her name to a brand of Champagne. The Dukes of Brissac gained their title as a reward for surrendering Paris to King Henri IV in 1594, thus helping to bring an end to the Wars of Religion. The guided tours could be livelier but at least a glass of the estate wine is offered at the end of the visit.
20km southeast of Angers off the D748. Tel: 41 91 22 21. Open: daily, July and August, 9am–7pm; Wednesday to Monday, April to June and September to November. Admission charge.

CHOLET

Cholet today is a centre for the manufacture of high-quality clothes and known for its independent, hard-working folk. The town was razed to the ground in 1794 during the brief and bloody Vendée Wars (see page 31) but the 'double red heart' badge of the region is still worn with pride and symbolic red handkerchiefs are sold in souvenir shops. Learn about the royalist cause in the Art and History Museum, opposite the town hall.
58km southwest of Angers on the N160. Musée d'Art et d'Histoire, Avenue de l'Abreuvoir. Tel: 41 49 29 00. Open: daily. Closed: Tuesday. Admission charge.

CLISSON

'A little bit of Italy on the Sèvre river' is one reaction to the town's square bell-towers, its loggias and its Roman-tile roofs. After fire destroyed the town during the Vendée Wars of 1794, two locals engaged the sculptor-architect Frédéric Lemot to rebuild their town. Even factory owners followed the pattern. Survivors of the fire include the handsome 15th-century covered market, a couple of bridges and the castle ruins atop a rocky outcrop. The summer music festival is first class.
90km southwest of Angers on the D763.

CUNAULT

Listen to Gregorian chant at Sunday mass to appreciate the atmosphere of this Romanesque priory church, built by 12th- and 13th-century Benedictine monks on the bank of the Loire. Pilgrims who crowded into the three naves can surely not have been able to decipher the carvings high up on the 223 pillars – bring binoculars if you want to do so. The usually quiet hamlet bustles with a

Above: Clisson's Italianate viaduct
Right: Clisson's ruined castle

craft market on Sunday mornings in summer.
40km southeast of Angers on the south bank of the Loire.

DOUÉ-LA-FONTAINE

Doué is nicknamed *La Cité des Roses* (the City of Roses) because over 8 million stems are grown here annually and shipped all over Europe. Some 500 varieties are found in the Parc Foulon and the air is scented by 100,000 blooms during the *Journées de la Rose*, the annual rose festival, in mid-July. The rose show takes place in a disused limestone quarry, now an amphitheatre; another series of old quarries has an unusually fine zoo (see page 154). In the former stables of a long-gone château is the Musée des Commerces Anciens, a museum of village shops. Much more interesting than it sounds, you can see how chemists once made pills by hand and find out why *tabacs* (tobacconists' shops) have a *carotte* (carrot-shaped sign) outside.
40km southeast of Angers on the D761.
Musée des Commerces Anciens, Ecuries Foulon-Soulanger. Tel: 41 59 28 23. Open: daily, March to Christmas; closed Monday. Admission charge.

LA FLÈCHE

'J'étais fléchois avant d'avoir été béarnais' ('I was from La Flèche before I was from Béarn'), insisted King Henri IV, who was conceived here in 1553 but born in Pau, in the south of France. In 1604, he founded the town's Jesuit college where his heart, along with that of his wife, Marie de'Medici, were interred in the chapel. Although their remains were exhumed and burnt during the French Revolution, the ashes were later found and are now set in a heart-shaped urn in the north transept. One of the college's first pupils was the philosopher René Descartes (1596–1650). When the Jesuits were expelled from France, the building became a military academy gaining its present reputation after Napoleon moved the Prytanée de St-Cyr military institution here in 1808. Many of the pupils go on to pursue a military career, and the graduates include over 800 generals.
52km northeast of Angers on the N23. Entrance on rue du Collège. Tel: 43 94 02 53. Open: daily. Admission charge. Proof of identity required for admission.

GOULAINE, CHÂTEAU DE

The Marquis de Goulaine's family have lived here for 1,000 years; the current château, however, dates back merely to the 15th century. Rooms such as the *Salon Bleu* are richly decorated and gleam with gilt.
90km southwest of Angers off the N249, 11km east of Nantes. Tel: 40 54 91 42. Open: weekends, Easter to October; daily mid-June to mid-September. Admission charge.

LOURESSE-ROCHEMENIER

Signposted as the Village Troglodytique de Rochemenier, this settlement consisted almost entirely of underground dwellings (see pages 74–5), carved out of the chalky limestone, until the 1930s, when the villagers built the present above-ground houses. The sunken farmsteads, houses and chapel have now been restored and a small museum shows the unromantic reality of underground life a century ago. An underground restaurant (see page 173) serves traditional *fouaces* (hot bread) straight from the oven.
40km southeast of Angers. Open: daily. Closed: Monday, except in July and August, and November to March. Admission charge.

MALICORNE-SUR-SARTHE

Pottery has been made here since Roman times, and the yellow or blue-patterned Malicorne pots, often depicting birds, are famous throughout France. A retrospective of this style, which dates from 1747, is in the Faïenceries d'Art museum. Step next door to see a dozen of today's *potiers* (potters) continue the hand-painting tradition.
53km northeast of Angers on the D23. Tel: 43 94 81 18. Open: daily, Easter to September; closed Monday.

MONTGEOFFROY, CHÂTEAU DE

The wrought iron gates fronting this charming château are crowned by the entwined initials of the de Contades family, owners of the Montgeoffroy estate since 1616. The 16th-century castle was remodelled by the Marshal de Contades in 1775 and scarcely anything has changed inside since – the fine furnishings, carpets and paintings remain in their original positions, giving an excellent idea of aristocratic life in the 18th century.
20km east of Angers off the N147 near Mazé. Tel: 41 80 60 02. Open: Easter to 1 November 9.30am–noon and 2.30–6.30pm. Admission charge.

Dining out: the Château de Montreuil-Bellay dominates the river Thouët

MONTREUIL-BELLAY, CHÂTEAU DE

This town on the Thouët river is dwarfed by its massive 17-towered château, with its reputation for impregnability. Like many other Loire Valley châteaux, it was revamped in the 15th century (originally built in 1025). The Harcourt family put in Turkish baths, better kitchens, 18 spiral staircases and a new chapel where frescoed angels, playing lutes and trumpets, flutter across the ceiling. On the front of the altar, a carving depicts a pregnant Virgin Mary meeting her cousin. Unlike some castles, the rooms are elegant and liveable. One of the most magnificent rooms in the château is the huge medieval kitchen with its central chimney and 18th-century cooking equipment. Equally impressive are the vaulted wine cellars, where the Confrérie de Sacavins (Brotherhood of Wine Growers) used to meet.

50km southeast of Angers on the N147. Tel: 41 52 33 06. Open: Wednesday to Monday, April to November. Admission charge.

Fixtures and fittings: Montgeoffroy is rich with antiques and paintings

NANTES AND NEARBY

The city that dominates the mouth of the Loire was traditionally the capital of Brittany. After the Revolution, it became the capital of the Loire-Atlantique region, and now it is the capital of the five disparate *départements* that make up the Pays de la Loire. After stagnating for most of this century, France's seventh largest city has been revived thanks to a bold programme of expansion and modernisation, carried out over the last 20 years.

Historically, Nantes was fought over by the French and the Breton dukes until Anne of Brittany, who was born here, married King Charles VIII, bringing Brittany under French rule in the 15th century. Nantes went on to become the country's largest port, made wealthy by the trade in slaves, sugar, rum and cotton. Decline followed the building of

Facelift: the old port of Nantes is being modernised and cleaned up

better facilities at nearby St-Nazaire, though, not before a young Jules Verne was inspired by the early 19th-century dockside to begin writing his adventure stories (he once ran away to sea, but only sailed downriver as far as Paimboeuf, now a pleasant little fishing harbour 40km to the west).

Around the river's mouth, the countryside is open and flat. The Lac de Grand-Lieu (to the north of the city) and the marshy Grande Brière nature park (to the west), are a paradise for birdwatchers. Few people live here now: traditional peat-cutting is restricted to a few days every August and the once-profitable salt pans have been converted to fish and oyster farms.

For many visitors the most memorable sight within the Nantes area is the 3.5km-long Pont de St-Nazaire bridge, which soars 60m above the Loire and links St-Nazaire to St-Brévin across the mouth of the river. Even Jules Verne did not anticipate this exhilarating experience.

Shop till you drop: boutiques in the Passage Pommeraye, Nantes

accentuated by dark and light stone. The original 11th-century fortress was partially destroyed during the Hundred Years' War; the keep and oak-panelled chapel are 15th- and 16th-century additions. Kings Louis XI, Charles VII, François I and Henri IV all stayed here, but the buildings were subsequently used as a farm for 200 years, and they fell into a state of near ruin until rescued and restored by the Countess Theobold Walsh in the 1870s (see page 40, Château de Serrant).
14km northwest of Angers off the N162. Tel: 41 32 67 93. Open: daily, March to November. Closed: Tuesday except in July and August. Admission charge.

PLESSIS-BOURRÉ, CHÂTEAU DU

With a turret at each corner, a moat and a drawbridge that is raised and lowered for visitors. Plessis-Bourré is as impressive now as it was when built in 1468 (see page 38). Completed just seven years later, it shows the transition from 'fortress' to Renaissance comfort. The royal finance minister, Jean Bourré, modelled it on Louis XI's château at Langeais where he supervised construction. Today, the rooms show changing styles in furnishings from the 15th to the 19th centuries.
18km north of Angers off the D52 and D109. Tel: 41 32 06 01. Open: July and August, 10am–6.30pm; mid-February to late June and September to late November, 10am–noon, 2–6.30pm (5pm in winter). Closed: Wednesday, and Thursday morning. Admission charge.

PLESSIS-MACÉ, CHÂTEAU DU

Plessis is a local term meaning 'palisade'. Unlike le Plessis-Bourré, built in just one architectural style, Macé is a mixture,

THE ENGLISH CONNECTION
Like Normandy, the Loire's historical links with England date from the time of William the Conqueror, crowned King of England in 1066. His great-grandson, Henri Plantagenet ruled Normandy, Anjou, Touraine and Maine. After marrying Eleanor of Aquitaine (see page 66), he controlled over half of France. In 1154, he became King Henry II of England. His death gave impetus to the rivalry between the monarchs of France and England that culminated in the Hundred Years' War, much of it fought in the Loire valley. A turning point came when Joan of Arc led the French to victory at Orléans in 1429. Even so, the English continued to rule parts of France until the loss of Calais in 1558, and did not finally cede their claims to French territory until 1801.

The Château du Plessis-Bourré, north of Angers (see page 37) was built in just seven years, so it is easy to follow the plan of the building and understand how the rooms were actually used. The 2m-thick walls and 44m-high *donjon* (keep) show that this was still, in part, a fortress, despite its early-Renaissance comforts.

Moats and Bridges

The château was built on a terrace, and was originally protected by no less than three moats. At the end of the 43m-long bridge, the restored drawbridge can be raised or lowered by one person in a matter of seconds, thanks to the 900kg counterbalance.

CHÂTEAU LIFE

room, 18th-century wood-panelling, painted the fashionable grey of the period, has replaced tapestry. The *Grand Salon* has fine 18th-century carvings on the walls but the *Salle de Parlement*, the vaulted ceremonial room, dates from an earlier period, when King Charles VIII and his sister, the regent Anne de Beaujeu, met ambassadors from Hungary here in 1487. The arms of the various monarchs who visited Plessis-Bourré, carved on the back of the door, show the owners' loyalty to the crown.

Despite its history and antiques, le Plessis-Bourré is still a family home

The Courtyard

Less austere than the exterior, the courtyard shows the influence of Renaissance ideas. On the west side, a covered walkway connects the main lodgings and the chapel; opposite are the servants' quarters and kitchens. The courtyard was large enough to host outdoor feasts, with musicians and jesters to entertain the guests.

Living Quarters

The height of the *Logis Seigneurial* (master's lodging) was designed to impress. On the ground floor, the *Vestibule d'Honneur* (entrance hall) has a massive fireplace, and the walls would have been hung with tapestries for additional insulation. In the Louis XVI

Upstairs, the *Salle des Gardes* was not actually the guard room. Instead, this heavily decorated room was the library of the owner Jean Bourré, whose fascination with alchemy prompted the allegorical figures painted on the 24 ceiling panels. Next door, the 19th-century Empire Room claims to have the only bed that Napoleon *never* slept in. The 35m-long Gallery was used for meeting, talking and doing business. At one end, the tiny *loggia* allowed the owner to attend mass without mixing with the servants in the chapel below.

Chapel of St Anne

All châteaux had their own chapel, with their own priests, and the encircled red crosses here indicate that this one is still consecrated. The obligatory statue of the local hero, St Martin, is in one corner.

Messing about on the river: the marina at Sablé-sur-Sarthe

SABLÉ-SUR-SARTHE

The Erve river joins the Sarthe here, and
a stretch of canalised river has been
turned into a marina where holiday craft
can be hired. There is also a river boat
for short cruises along the Sarthe. Above
stands the proud château where 19th-
century inventor Charles Cros conducted
his experiments. It now houses an
annexe of the National Library of
France. The attractive town is known for
its shortbread-like biscuits.
*64km northeast of Angers off the A11
and D306.*

ST-FLORENT-LE-VIEIL

The small town perched above the Loire
has two claims to fame: it is the place
where the Vendée Wars began in 1793
and it is the resting place of the royalist
leader, General Bonchamps (see page
31). His romantic white marble effigy was
a moving 'thank you' from the sculptor,
David d'Angers, whose father was one of
5,000 prisoners saved from slaughter by
Bonchamps. Today the church hosts a
music festival in June and July.
*42km west of Angers off the N23 and D752.
Tel: 41 72 62 32 for festival details.*

ST-GEORGES-SUR-LOIRE
Château de Serrant

This château is one of two in the region
(see the Château de Plessis-Macé, page
37) associated with the Walsh family,
Irish Jacobites descended from Captain
Francis Walsh who helped King James II
escape to France when he was deposed
from the English throne by William III of
Orange in 1688. Walsh settled in Nantes
and grew rich as a merchant and
shipowner. His son, Antoine,

General Bonchamps at St-Florent-le-Vieil

subsequently provided the frigate, *La Doutelle*, used by Bonnie Prince Charlie in 1745 for his disastrous attempt to retake the Scottish and English thrones. In 1749, the Walsh family bought this château, and though it passed to the family of the present owner, Prince Jean-Charles de Ligne, in 1830, there are reminders of the Walsh connection in the magnificent library, with its 12,000 volumes. Begun in 1546, it took another 200 years to complete the château, but the builders remained faithful to the original plan. The result is a gem of geometry, balanced and photogenic, with gravelled paths, a moat and domed turrets. The furnishings are exceptional, so this château is well worth seeing inside.
1km northeast of St-Georges-sur-Loire. Tel: 41 39 13 01. Open: daily, 28 March to 1 November. Closed: Tuesday except in July and August. Admission charge.

St-Georges-sur-Loire is 18km west of Angers on the N23.

ST-HILAIRE-ST-FLORENT

Wedged between tufa cliffs and the Thouët river, this is the main production centre for sparkling Saumur wine. Many of the labyrinthine rock galleries where the wine is stored can be visited (see page 144). There are also two museums (of mushrooms and masks, see pages 156–7) while on the plateau above the town is the famous national riding school, L'Ecole Nationale d'Equitation (see page 157).
48km southeast of Angers on the D751. Musée du Champignon, La Houssaye. Tel: 41 50 31 55.

ST-LAMBERT-DU-LATTAY

This unremarkable village is the production centre for the Coteaux du Layon dessert wine. All is explained in the

small museum. Take the smell test; good noses win a certificate.
15km southwest of Angers on the N160. Musée de la Vigne et du Vin d'Anjou. Tel: 41 78 42 75. Open: daily, April to October. Admission charge.

ST-LAURENT-DE-LA-PLAINE

When villagers stop weaving or making clogs and wine the old-fashioned way, their tools are usually thrown out. Luckily, the locals here kept their tools and opened an imaginative crafts museum representing some 50 trades. A 'village street' shows the younger generation how the blacksmith and candle-maker worked. Everything comes to life in July and August when live crafts demonstrations are given. Entertaining as well as educational for youngsters.
26km southwest of Angers off the N160 and D170. La Musée des Vieux Métiers. Tel: 41 78 24 08. Open: daily, April to November. Admission charge.

Mask museum at St-Hilaire-St-Florent

SAUMUR

Saumur became an important Protestant enclave after the ambitious 16th-century governor Duplessis-Mornay (nicknamed 'the Huguenot pope') founded a college that attracted Protestants from all over Europe. Industrious Huguenot businessmen soon followed and the city prospered until the revocation of the Edict of Nantes (see page 59) when much of the population fled. The arrival of the cavalry (see page 44) brought a revival. Since then wine, mushrooms and the army have underpinned the economy. With its old quarter, its grandiose and newly renovated town hall, its small shops and its château, Saumur is one of the most attractive towns in the region.

Le château

Straight and severe, Saumur's medieval fortress enjoys views that stretch for 20km up, down and across the Loire Valley. Horses once clattered up the steep drawbridge; the smooth side ramp was for barrels. Inside are small museums of ceramics, furniture and religious art. Most interesting, however, are the castle's bottom and top: a real dungeon, 24 spiral steps down in the gloom, and, up under the eaves, a museum of the horse, with saddles from Iran to Mexico, plus uniforms, boots weighing 2kg each and even an equine skeleton.

Tel: 41 51 30 46. Open: daily. Closed: Tuesday from October to March. Admission charge.

Le Dolmen de Bagneux

The Great Dolmen of Bagneux is one of Europe's largest prehistoric chamber tombs, but the setting, in a garden with entry via a café, is less than impressive.

Bird's-eye view: the town of Saumur from the château ramparts

Slate mining: the Trélazé coat of arms

56 rue de Dolmen, Bagneux. Tel: 41 50 23 02. Open: daily. Admission charge.

Notre-Dame de Nantilly
This fine 12th-century Romanesque church is hung with 15th- to 17th-century tapestries depicting scenes from the lives of Christ and the Virgin. Also notable is the epitaph to Lady Thyphaine, supposedly composed by Good King Réné (see page 27) as a tribute to his wet-nurse.
rue de Nantilly.

Musée des Blindés (Tank Museum) and Musée de l'Ecole de Cavalerie (Cavalry Museum)
See pages 156–7.

SOLESMES ABBEY
This Benedictine abbey, founded in 1010, was closed at the Revolution but reoccupied by a new community of monks in 1833, to become the headquarters of the French Benedictines in 1837 and a major force in the revival of Gregorian chant. With its 50m-high walls, it looks more like a fortress than a retreat but the medieval style is largely a 19th-century creation. Only the abbey church of St-Pierre is open to the public. In the transept are the very fine 16th-century sculptural groups known as the 'Solesmes Saints'. These depict scenes from the life of the Virgin. Jean Bougler, the 16th-century prior who commissioned the work, is depicted in the crowded Entombment scene, holding the Virgin's shroud.
65km northeast of Angers off the A11 and D306, not far from Sablé. Tel: 43 95 00 60. Open: daily, with services at 9.45am and 1, 1.50, 5 and 8.30pm. Donation appreciated.

TRÉLAZÉ
For centuries, the slate centre of France provided roofing for cathedrals and châteaux. Undercut by cheaper competition, slate is quarried nowadays only for renovating historic buildings. At the Slate Museum, retired *ardoisiers* (slate workers), wearing clogs on their feet and cloths round their legs, demonstrate how to convert a ton of rock into grey-blue wafers. Tools, machines and slate carvings are also on show.
5km southeast of Angers off the D952. Musée de l'Ardoise. Tel: 41 69 04 71. Open: Tuesday to Sunday, July to mid-September at 2pm; rest of year, Sundays and public holidays only at 2pm. Admission charge.

SAUMUR'S HORSES

The partnership of Saumur and horses dates back to the 16th century when the Protestant university opened and a Monsieur de St-Vual set up a riding academy alongside. Then, when the French cavalry was reorganised by the Duke de Choiseul, in 1763, he chose Saumur as the site of the new training school for officers.

The French Revolution put a temporary stop to this élitism, but the Royal School of Cavalry reopened early in the 19th century, with the Cadre Noir squad of officers formed in 1814. An early riding master designed the handsome all-black uniform that is still worn today, trimmed with gold braid and topped by a *lampion* (cocked hat). In 1828, the young officers celebrated their graduation for the first time with a public exhibition of equestrian skill, known as the *carrousel*.

The *carrousel* is still the most famous of the displays but, between April and September, thousands also watch the *Reprise du Manège*, a balletic dressage and the *Reprise des Sauteurs*, when the horses and riders perform a series of gravity-defying jumps, similar to a gymnast's floor exercises. You don't have to be an equine enthusiast to admire the skills of the horses, or of the men, who ride without the benefit of stirrups.

Since 1972, the school (now the Ecole Nationale d'Equitation) has come under the government's Sports' Ministry, and among the 450 horses

Saumur has strong claims to be the equestrian capital of France

and 200 pupils are Olympic show-jumpers and three-day event horses, carriage drivers and dressage riders, all being trained under the watchful eye of 45 staff, 20 of whom are members of the illustrious Cadre Noir.

Even if you can't see horses in action, you can always visit the Cavalry School Museum, tracing the history of the French cavalry since the 18th century.

Avenue Foch. Tel: 41 51 05 43, ext 306. Open: Tuesday, Wednesday and Thursday, 9am–noon, 2–5pm, Sunday, 2–5pm. Guided tours are also given from March to September of the Ecole Nationale d'Equitation (for information on tours and displays, tel: 41 50 21 35, ext 381).

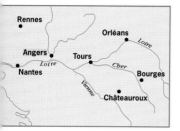

Old Angers

Much of old Angers has been pedestrianised, so a stroll through the heart of this 'city of art and history' is particularly enjoyable. *Allow one hour.*

Start at the tourist office in front of the castle (place du Président Kennedy). Turn right on rue Toussaint, known for its antique shops. The brick and stone wall on the left was built by the Romans some 1,800 years ago.

1 ABBAYE DE TOUSSAINT

On the right-hand side (No 37) is an entrance to a monastic courtyard now used for concerts. Turn left inside and pass along the cloister to what remains of the 13th-century abbey church. Now restored, its dramatic modern glass roof soars above sculptures in the Galerie David d'Angers (see page 29). *Climb the steps and turn right, continuing along rue Toussaint. Number 25, 'built by knowledge and fortified by wisdom', was restored in 1588. Turn right on the cobbled rue du Musée.*

2 MUSÉE DES BEAUX-ARTS

Step into the courtyard on the right and look up to see late 15th-century gargoyles. Built as a private mansion, it was once Le Logis Barrault (see page 30).

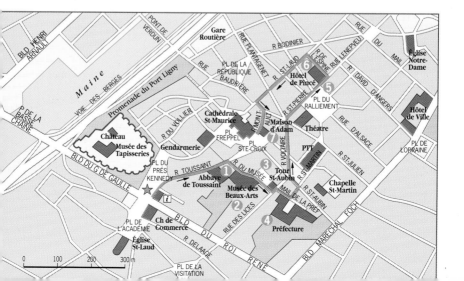

The Musée des Beaux-Arts, Angers

Continue along rue du Musée, noting the mix of black slate and white limestone in the wall. The bridge overhead linked two seminaries, one in the mansion, the other in the church of St Eloi.

3 TOUR ST-AUBIN
The 55m-high belfry (and the cloister in the Préfecture – see below) are all that remain of the powerful Benedictine Abbey of St-Aubin. The tower originally stood outside the city walls; the opening 4m up was reached by a ladder, which was then drawn up for safety.
Cross rue des Lices, where knights once held tournaments, and enter the Mail de la Préfecture.

4 PRÉFECTURE
This is the headquarters of the *département* of Maine-et-Loire. Members of the public may go in to see the remarkable Romanesque cloister with its sculptures and its frescos of David and Goliath, Herod and the Three Kings.
Exit on rue St-Martin and turn left on rue St-Aubin, looking up to see the cathedral's towers. Turn right, at the red British telephone box, on rue Voltaire. Turn right on rue St-Pierre.

5 PLACE DU RALLIEMENT
Some say this was the site of patriotic rallies during the French Revolution, others that the crowds met to watch executions at the guillotine. Entertainment is now provided in the theatre, built in 1871 and recently restored. The façade is decorated with busts of France's famous French playwrights, such as Molière, Racine and Corneille.
Continue along rue Lenepveu.

6 HÔTEL DE PINCÉ
Gargoyles and foliage carvings decorate this 16th-century mansion, now the Turpin de Crissé Museum of Greek, Etruscan and Egyptian antiquities, and Japanese and Chinese art.
Turn left on rue de l'Espine, named after the architect of the Hôtel de Pincé, and left again on rue St-Laud. Stop at No 21 to see the 15th-century carvings of Adam and Eve, plus a beast swallowing a bear. The nightclub at No 38, in delightful art nouveau style, was once a brothel. Pass the modern shopping centre and turn left on rue de l'Oisellerie, pausing to admire the three old houses. On the right is the former bishop's palace. Turn right on rue Montault.

7 MAISON D'ADAM
Heavily timbered gables were a sign of wealth; the decoration is in the flamboyant Gothic style. Spot the pelican feeding its chicks, Samson fighting the lion and the man with three testicles (see page 29).
The walk ends in the place Ste-Croix where you can visit the cathedral (see page 28).

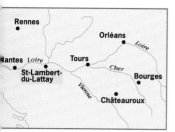

Cycling in the Layon Valley

The Layon is a relatively unknown tributary of the Loire; local vineyards produce Côteaux du Layon, sweet white wines drunk by the locals as an aperitif, with dessert or even right through a meal. Although not long, this is a testing route, best done by mountain bike. *Allow half a day, longer if you take the optional canoe trip on the Layon river.*

Start from St-Lambert-du-Lattay, where the tourist office (tel: 41 78 44 26) rents bicycles and has mapped out several trails, marked with red, green or blue arrows.

1 ST-LAMBERT-DU-LATTAY
Straddling the busy N160, this village boasts 50 winegrowers

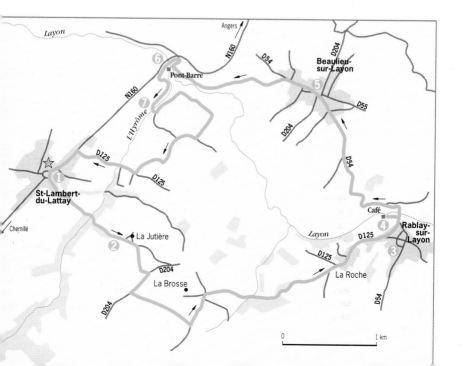

whose skills are explained in the Musée de la Vigne et du Vin (see page 41). Near by, the Maison du Vin sells the local red, white and rosé wines, and the sweet Côteaux du Layon (open: April to September).

Start in the main square by the Maison du Vin. Follow markers for the tourist office's 'red route' to La Roche.

2 THE VINEYARDS

The trail descends steeply past a pond and campsite; follow the arrows pointing to a rough path through the vines. Note the information board explaining the varieties of grapes grown here, including *groslot* for making Rosé d'Anjou.

Cross the bridge. Except for bird song and the distant church clock, silence reigns. The path passes oak trees and nettles, sloe bushes and thistle; continue through vineyards and maize fields. Beyond the hamlet of La Roche, leave the tourist board's route and follow signs to Rablay-sur-Layon.

3 RABLAY-SUR-LAYON

This 'artists' community', home to various painters, sculptors and artisans, remains pleasantly uncommercial, with Le Mail, an atmospheric small square, and an ancient Maison de la Dîme (tithe house).

Return to the tourist board route at the edge of La Roche. At the side of the building on the right, signposted, 'Domaine des Quarres, Vignoble Bidet', take the rough trail down to the valley floor.

4 FROM PEDAL TO PADDLE

Follow the Layon river to a *guingette* (snack bar) which also rents canoes and kayaks in summer (weekends in April, May and September; daily in June, July and August). Paddle upstream, past gardens, houses and fields.

Resume the cycle ride, crossing the bridge. Do not turn off on to the 'red route'. Follow the D54 up the steep hill to Beaulieu-sur-Layon.

5 BEAULIEU-SUR-LAYON

This ancient village thrived in the 19th century, thanks to nearby coal mines and limeworks; now it is known for its wines and flowers.

Just beyond the tourist office, turn sharp left on the rue du Square. Pick up the 'red route' again, heading back down to the river. Turn right and follow the bankside path to the old bridge.

6 PONT-BARRE

'Ici commence le pays de la Guerre des Géants' (The land of the Giants' War starts here) – so says the plaque commemorating the 2,000 soldiers who died here on 19 September, 1793, in the Vendée Wars (see page 31). The peasant-soldiers were dubbed 'the Giants' by Napoleon Bonaparte when 3,000 of them defeated his 25,000-strong army.

Cross the bridge and join the 'green route' into the Hyrôme valley.

7 HYRÔME VALLEY

After about 1km, on the left, there is a carved stone tablet under a chestnut tree recalling the days when eight watermills dotted the banks of the river. Now the valley is enjoyed by nature lovers, ramblers and cyclists.

Return to St-Lambert via the D125.

Cruising the Mayenne

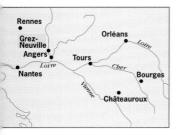

Although boating on the Mayenne is popular, this particular stretch of the river is remarkably unspoilt. *Allow two days for the return journey, and one day if you arrange for your boat to be collected at the end of the one-way journey.*

1 GREZ-NEUVILLE

As well as a small island, old mill and a weir, this pretty village has a marina full of *pénichettes* – cruising boats with wide decks, guard rails and a practical wheel house, set well back. Rent them from L'Anjou Plaisance; bicycles are usually supplied with the boats (tel: 41 95 68 95). No permit is required. *Head upstream (north), passing the first lock (No 42) on the left. After a few minutes, the Oudon river also flows in from the left. Head beneath the bridge at the river junction, and up the Oudon for 1.5km.*

2 LE LION D'ANGERS

On the right, the Isle-Briand is one of France's best-known national studs with 75 thoroughbred stallions, plus a fine race course. Watch for horses in training. (Guided visits in the afternoon. Tel: 41 95 82 46.) *Return to the Mayenne, continue upstream.*

3 MONTREUIL-SUR-MAINE

Thick trees line both banks, but at Montreuil, the church spire pokes out above the greenery. *The second lock (No 41) is at Montreuil, and a small, elegant country house peeks through the trees on the left. The third lock (No 40), at La Roche Chambellay, takes boats to the left, between the bank and a small island. Look across the fields to the church spire in Chambellay.*

Grez-Neuville is a good starting point for exploring the Mayenne river

4 CHAMBELLAY

A distinctive five-arched bridge carries the D290 across the river. Some enthusiasts moor here and pedal 2km to look at the 15th-century Château de Bois-Montbourcher (not open to the public). Others pop into the church to see the frescos.
Continue upstream.

5 CHENILLÉ-CHANGÉ

This base for cruising boats is lit up at night and boasts of being voted France's prettiest 'flowery' village in 1989. Even the pink lock-keeper's cottage has a manicured garden. The old watermill still functions, although it is now a restaurant, La Table du Meunier.
Continue upstream for about 3km to La Jaille-Yvon.

6 LA JAILLE-YVON

This village is hidden from view on a bluff, 50m above the water. From the campsite at the foot of the cliff, climb up to the 11th-century church for a sweeping view over the countryside.
Continue upstream via Lock No 38, past the château at Le Port-Joulain, a popular stretch for water-skiers.

7 DAON

Everyone seems to be having fun in this little resort where the flags of eight nations flap on the modern bridge. L'Embarcadère restaurant, on the water, specialises in grilled meat and fish.
Beyond Daon, the lock at Formusson (No 37) has charts showing local bird life.
Now the Mayenne narrows to form an ox-bow bend, with chestnuts and hazels hiding the Château de Magnanne on the left bank.

8 MÉNIL

In this charming hamlet, an old-fashioned, hand-powered *bac* (ferry) takes pedestrians and bicycles to and fro.
Three more locks (Nos 36, 35 and 34) lead into the affluent town of Château-Gontier.

9 CHÂTEAU-GONTIER

Handsome quayside gardens greet boaters; even the tourist office is housed in a converted boat. The 11th-century church of St-Jean-Baptiste is a treasure and the old town has many half-timbered houses.
Continue upstream to the rural peace of Mirwault where the Hostellerie de Mirwault is a fine place to celebrate the half-way point, or the end, of the journey.

West Central Loire

Most of the Loire Valley's most famous châteaux are located in this region, even if most are on other rivers, such as the Cher, the Indre and the Vienne. Some date back 900 years to the era of Foulques III Nerra, Count of Anjou, who was a prolific builder of fortresses (see page 71). In later centuries, these châteaux were strengthened as protection against the English, particularly during the Hundred Years' War.

The end of the war, in 1453, marked the start of the transition from the 'military' to the 'domestic' style in château architecture. Down came the bleak walls and up went the living quarters with their large windows and sweeping staircases. Terraces and gardens were made in the Italian style. The 15th and 16th centuries were the era of the 'Royal Loire', when the kings and queens of France held court here, only two day's ride from Paris, and their followers built châteaux near by.

Each of the châteaux has its own appeal. Amboise oozes history, and is being restored to the regal appearance it had when it was home to five French kings. Azay-le-Rideau is a thing of beauty, mirrored in a

moat that was built for aesthetic reasons, not defensive. The fascinating astrologer's room at Chaumont recalls Catherine de'Medici and her plots to overthrow her rivals, particularly Diane de Poitiers, owner of nearby Chenonceau, arching across the Cher river.

Some châteaux witnessed important events in French history. At Chinon, Joan of Arc convinced Charles VII that she could boot the English out of France (see page 92). In the equally sombre Langeais, Charles VIII's marriage to Anne of Brittany brought the Bretons under the French flag. Loches may have chilling dungeons, but the beauty of Agnès Sorel, the first 'official' royal mistress still haunts the castle. The Sleeping Beauty of Ussé is imaginary, the creation of fairy-tale author Charles Perrault, while at Villandry, the main attraction

Coat of arms, Langeais

WEST CENTRAL LOIRE

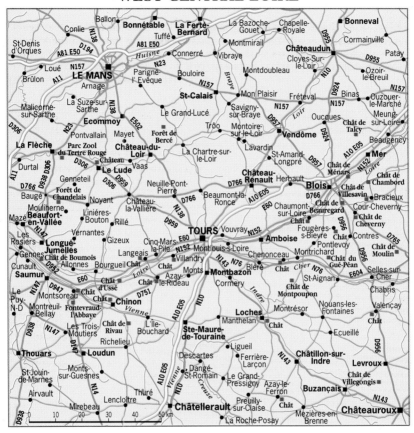

is down-to-earth: the formal gardens.

Not everything is on a grand scale. The valley of Le Loir river has romantic villages. The town of Richelieu was an early example of urban planning. There are shrines to three of France's greatest writers: the poet Pierre de Ronsard, who lived at the priory of St-Cosme en l'Isle François on the outskirts of Tours; the

novelist Honoré de Balzac, who wrote at Saché; and Rabelais, who grew up at La Devinière and drank with his friends in Chinon. Then there was artist and inventor Leonardo da Vinci, who lived out his last days at Le Clos-Lucé in Amboise. All this, plus the medieval cathedral city of Tours, ensures plenty of choice for the vistor.

Tours

*M*otorists on the A10 motorway, speeding past this city of 250,000 people, ee modern factories, sprawling suburbs and, very briefly, the River Loire. They miss the Gallo-Roman walls, the medieval stained glass in the Cathedral of St-Gatien, scores of half-timbered and Renaissance buildings and some unusual small museums. All of this lies within a compact city centre full of restaurants, shops and students.

The city became known as Tours, after the Turones, the Gallic tribe who settled on the north bank of the Loire, instead of keeping its Roman name, *Caesarodunum* (Caesar's Hill). Even so, the Roman site, set between the Loire and Cher rivers, is the base of today's city. Although nothing remains of the amphitheatre, where thousands of spectators once cheered their heroes, portions of brick and stone Gallo-Roman walls still stand by the river and off rue des Ursulines, not far from the cathedral. A separate district, called Chateauneuf (or Martinopolis), stands to the west and dates from the 5th century. The focus here was the early-Christian basilica, with the shrine of St Martin, bishop of Tours.

When (in 1461) King Louis XI built his château at Plessis-lès-Tours (see page 73), 3km west of this basilica, the city prospered greatly, becoming known for its silk and gold-embroidered fabrics. Its mint already produced the official currency, the *denier tournois*. The 16th-century Wars of Religion signalled the end of the glory days and Tours sank into provincialism. By the early 19th century, its population of 20,000 was less than that of Angers or Orléans.

Like many other French cities, Tours was badly damaged during World War II, but the past 35 years have seen the old city rebuilt, thanks to the efforts of the long-standing Mayor, Jean Royer. Yet Tours is no living museum. Balancing the large numbers of professionals who live here is the large population of students attending the university and its two

Upstairs, downstairs: rue Briçonnet in the Quartier Plumereau

international language schools.

'*La douceur de vivre existe toujours*' (Here, the good life still goes on) is how one Tours resident sums up the attractions of the liveliest city on the Loire. It is also known as 'petit Paris' because Victor Laloux, the architect of the Gare d'Orsay in the capital (now the Musée d'Orsay) also designed the railway station in Tours, the town hall and the new basilica of St Martin. So what if the city is cut in half by the RN10, the main Paris to Bordeaux road? That simply makes the city's rue Nationale 'the longest boulevard in Europe'. This same optimism applies to the renovation of the cathedral, due to finish in time for the papal visit in 1997, marking the 1,600th anniversary of St Martin's death.

The heart of old Tours

TOURS

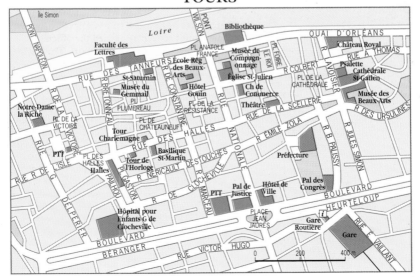

La Basilique St-Martin

A strong imagination is required to visualise the enormous 11th-century basilica that once stretched westwards from place de Châteauneuf to the Tour de l'Horloge (Clock Tower). Sacked during the Wars of Religion, it collapsed during the Revolution and was cleared in 1802 to make way for the rue des Halles. Of the original basilica, the rebuilt Tour Charlemagne (the former north transept) is stark and dull, surrounded by weeds and fenced in from traffic. St Martin himself is more revered by foreigners than by the French, and

visiting pilgrims still come to see the shrine in the crypt of the new basilica (1886–1924), built in neo-Byzantine style partly over the site of St Martin's original 5th-century tomb. Around the corner, the Musée St-Martin tells the story of the saint.

Museum: 3 rue Rapin. Tel: 47 64 48 87. Open: mid-March to mid-November, Wednesday to Sunday. Admission charge.

Cathédrale de St-Gatien

This striking building illustrates the development of the Gothic style, from the mid-13th to the 16th century; to the layman, that means that the architecture ranges from the starkly simple style of the chancel to the flamboyant west front, whose twin towers are crowned with delicate tracery. The current restoration project aims to restore the rich carvings as well as the creamy whiteness of the stone.

To the left of the façade are foundation walls dating from the Gallo-Roman period (late 3rd century). It was about this time that St Gatien and St Martin first began preaching the message of Christianity to the people of Tours. St Martin's story is told in the 13th-century stained-glass windows in a chapel off the ambulatory. Beginning at the bottom, these show: St Martin giving half of his cloak to a beggar, then seeing Christ in his cloak; the accident-prone saint being saved by a gold-winged angel from a cheeky devil trying to trip him, then being saved from crushing by a pine tree. Then, on the right, his body is shown being rowed upstream from the abbey at Candes-St-Martin (see page 72) to Tours, a reference to the legend that St

This rose window in St-Gatien's Cathedral is 600 years old

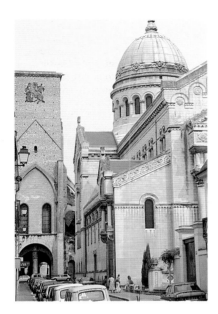

was imprisoned here after his father's assassination (see page 59). Note the height of the window: the boy is said to have jumped from here to freedom. In the Logis de Mars at the foot of the tower are the Musée Grévin waxworks (depicting important moments in the city's history, see page 157) and the Aquarium.

Museum: quai d'Orléans. Tel: 47 61 02 95.
Open: daily, mid-November to mid-March
2–5.30pm only. Admission charge.

Left: ancient tower, modern basilica
Below: St-Gatien's Cathedral

Martin's remains were snatched from Candes by the monks of Tours.

To the south of the choir is the sad tomb of the children of Charles VIII and Anne of Brittany, all of whom died in infancy. Their doll-like effigies are guarded by carved angels. Balzac used the Psalette, or choir school, as the setting for his novel, *Le Curé de Tours*. Protruding from the north flank of the cathedral the sheltering cloisters form a rectangle where choristers would meet. Above the cloisters, energetic-looking gargoyles contrast with the delicacy of the Renaissance staircase.
place de la Cathédrale.

Château Royal
All that remains of this 13th-century medieval fortress are two towers. The Tour de Guise, nearest the river, is named for the young Duke de Guise who

Eglise St-Julien

This new church was started in 970 after the Vikings destroyed the original, founded by historian-bishop Gregory of Tours in 575. Despite damage during the Wars of Religion, the Revolution and World War II, an 11th-century belfry porch remains, its capitals carved with stags, birds and two dogs holding a man upside down. In the chapter house is the Musée des Vins de Touraine (Touraine Wine Museum). The cloister houses the Musée du Compagnonnage (Trade Guild Museum), displaying hundreds of 'exam' pieces made by apprentices, from satin wedding shoes to a scale model of Milan cathedral (see page 157).
rue Nationale. Musée des Vins de Touraine. Tel: 47 61 02 95. Open: Wednesday to Monday. Musée du Compagnonnage. Tel: 47 61 07 93. Open: Wednesday to Monday. Admission charge for both.

Musée des Beaux-Arts de Tours

The Fine Arts Museum is housed in the 17th-century archbishop's palace, from where there are fine views of the cathedral, especially from the entrance and from Room 9 upstairs. In the Salle de la Régence, locally made red silk brocade recalls Tours' reputation for fine fabrics. Fans of local author, Honoré de Balzac (1799–1850) should climb to the top floor to see his portrait and romantic statue by Rodin, along with a mobile by American kinetic artist Alexander Calder (1898–1976) who, like Balzac, spent some time in Saché (see page 76).
18 place François Sicard. Tel: 47 05 68 73. Open: Wednesday to Monday. Admission charge.

Musée du Gemmail

A cross between *gemmes* (gems) and *émail* (enamel), this 50-year-old art form faithfully reproduces famous paintings on glass. The best are signed by Picasso, Braque and Rouault. A mini-workshop demonstrates the technique.
Hôtel Raimhault, 7 rue du Mûrier. Tel: 47 61 01 19. Open: May to mid-October, Tuesday to Sunday. Admission charge.

Quartier St-Julien

Rue Colbert is the main street of the characterful St-Julien district, now an area of art galleries and antique shops. Heading eastwards, look out for No 27, with its carved faces and figures, and at No 39, where a wrought-iron image of 'La Pucelle Armée' (The Armed Maiden) hangs above a shoe shop; according to legend, Joan of Arc's armour was made in a house on this site. Cross the rue Voltaire. Further on is No 64 alongside the alley named the Passage du Coeur Navré (Heartbreak Alley), so-called because it was the route to the gallows on place Foire-le-Roi.

THE WARS OF RELIGION (1562–98)

The 16th century brought the creative flowering of the Renaissance to France. It also saw 36 years of religious conflict between Catholics and Huguenots (the name given to followers of John Calvin, the French Protestant leader).

In 1560, a group of Huguenots tried to petition the young Francis II for religious freedom – or were they planning his kidnap? When word got out, the court moved from Blois to the greater safety of Amboise. There, the so-called 'Amboise Conspiracy' was foiled and the alleged plotters were caught and either beheaded, drawn and quartered, or hanged from the balcony.

The wars started in earnest after the slaughter of numerous Huguenots in

Medieval domestic architecture still survives in the place Plumereau

Wassy in 1562; in later years, thousands more died – in massacres in Angers, Orléans and Paris and during the 200-day siege of Sancerre. In revenge, the Huguenots sacked abbeys and churches, such as Beaugency, Marmoutiers and the Basilica of St Martin in Tours. At St-Benoît, the fine library was looted, while at Orléans, zealous Huguenots blew up the cathedral tower and most of the nave.

Henri III (1551–89) was caught between the extreme Catholic League, headed by Henri, Duke of Guise and the Protestants, led by Henri of Navarre. When the Guise faction threatened to usurp the throne, the king took the ultimate sanction: on 23 December, 1588, his men murdered the Duke of Guise at Blois. Several months later, King Henri III was himself assassinated by a fanatical Catholic, bringing an end to the Valois line of kings.

In the search for a successor, moderate Catholics supported Henri of Navarre who, in turn, converted to Catholicism (saying 'Paris is well worth a mass') and in 1589, he was crowned Henri IV. In 1598, he issued the Edict of Nantes, granting the Huguenots equal political rights and limited freedom of worship. The result was 70 years of peace, though Louis XIV revoked the Edict in 1685. He forbade Protestant worship and, although he closed the borders, some 50,000 families, including military leaders, wealthy bankers and merchants, university professors and highly skilled weavers left France forever, taking their money and know-how to more sympathetic countries.

AMBOISE

Despite mass tourism this is a delightful town, full of bustle and kept looking smart, thanks to an ongoing renovation programme. Leave the car in the main parking area by the river bank, where there is a large frog fountain by the Surrealist sculptor, Max Ernst (1891–1976). The rue François I leads past the Hôtel de Ville (Town Hall), with its statue of Louis XI in the courtyard, to the newly pedestrianised place du Château.

The Château

Here, too, restoration continues on what remains of the château complex, large parts of which were demolished in the early 19th century, and damaged during World War II. A royal residence between 1434 and 1560, its splendour was due to two monarchs. Charles VIII, born here in 1470, brought the lifestyle of the Renaissance back from Italy and, with his queen, Anne of Brittany, started an ambitious building programme. He died suddenly at the age of 28, after hitting his

SITES ET MONUMENTS HISTORIQUES
LE CLOS LUCÉ
où mourut
Léonard de Vinci

Renaissance man: Leonardo da Vinci spent his last years in Amboise

head on a low doorway. Work continued under François I who persuaded Leonardo da Vinci to move from his native Italy and live near by at Clos-Lucé as chief painter, architect and engineer to the king.

Inside, the most interesting room is the Salle des Etats (the Hall of States), with its double Gothic naves and slender columns. Note the coats of arms of France and Brittany and the ermine, symbol of Queen Anne. Look out, too, for the Conspirators' Balcony: after the attempted 'kidnap' of King François II (see page 58), the conspirators were hung from the balustrade or beheaded below.

Before entering the Chapelle de St-Hubert, stop to admire the carvings above the door. Charles VIII and Queen Anne are shown kneeling either side of the Virgin and Child, while below is a frieze showing St Hubert, patron saint of hunters, stunned by his vision of the Crucified Christ which appears between the antlers of a stag.

The Tour des Minimes was built with a 185m-long spiral ramp to enable cavalrymen to ride up to the castle from the riverside. Visitors can see only part of it but, in summer, they can walk down to the town through the Tour Heurtault, which has a similar ramp, and fine vault carvings.

Tel: 47 57 00 98. Open: daily. Admission charge.
Son et Lumière show from late June to early September (tel: 47 57 14 47 for details).

Le Clos-Lucé

Léonardo da Vinci (1452–1519) spent the last three years of his life in this red-brick manor house, situated just south of the château. The basement now houses a display of 40 models based on his inventions, ranging from tanks and fan-shaped guns to a swing bridge and even a flying machine.
rue Victor-Hugo. Tel: 47 57 62 88. Open: daily. Admission charge.

Amboise is 24km east of Tours, on the south bank of the Loire.

AZAY-LE-RIDEAU

Like two beauty queens, Azay and Chenonceau compete for the title of 'most beautiful château on water'. Both are described as 'feminine' because they were commissioned by women, but their elegance is typically Renaissance. The turreted towers are for trysts rather than sentry duty, while the machicolations look like a border of crimped pastry. Built on the Indre river, the name comes from Ridel or Rideau d'Azay, a 12th-century knight, but the present château was built by a mayor of Tours, the financier Gilles Berthelot – or rather by his wife, Philippa Lesbahy, who supervised the work.

In 1527, after a scandal, the château was taken over by François I. His emblem, the fire-breathing salamander, is carved above the fireplace in the Chambre du Roi (the King's Chamber) as well as on the front of the building, followed by his wife's symbol, the ermine. Despite several grand staircases the interior is less impressive than the lovely exterior, reflected in its mirror-like moat.
26km southwest of Tours on the D751.
Tel: 47 45 42 04. Open: daily. Admission charge.
Son et Lumière show: evenings end of May to end of September (tel: 47 45 44 40 for information).

Feminine touch: Philippa Lesbahy helped design Azay-le-Rideau

CHAUMONT-SUR-LOIRE

The sight of the fortified entrance to this château is worth the 200m uphill walk. Cross the drawbridge slowly, playing 'spot the symbol': the volcano (or *chaud mont* – hot mountain is the emblem of the castle. At eye level, the intertwined 'C's refer to owner Charles d'Amboise and his wife, Catherine; the 'D', alternating with a bow, horn and quiver stands for Diane de Poitiers, the favourite of King Henri II (see page 67).

Like many state-owned châteaux, it is sparsely furnished and you may be content to view the exterior architecture. Standing on the castle terrace it is possible to appreciate the commanding position of this site. For once, the original fort was not built by the legendary Foulques III Nerra (see page 71), but by his brother-in-law as a defence against him. Today's structure dates mainly from the period 1465 to

1510, though later owners put in large windows and pulled down the north wing to open up the view.

Inside, there is a collection of 18th-century medallion portraits, including one of the bespectacled American inventor, Benjamin Franklin. The Italian artist, J B Nini, worked in a pottery in the stables. More carved symbols decorate the massive fireplace in the dining room, while the floor in the council chamber is covered in 17th-century Italian tiles, put in a century ago. Although legend has it that Catherine de'Medici's astrologer, Ruggieri, foretold the deaths of her sons and the end of the Valois dynasty, his room is rather lacking in supernatural atmosphere.

47km east of Tours on the N751. Tel: 54 20 98 03. Open: daily. Admission charge.

CHENONCEAU

'*S'il vient à point, me souviendra*' (When it's finished, they'll remember me) reads the inscription over the entrance. Sadly, few do think of Thomas Bohier, the château's early-16th-century owner. Most focus on its feminine mystique. Bohier's wife, Catherine Briçonnet, oversaw the initial building work, which was extended by Diane de Poitiers, mistress of King Henri II and rival of his queen, Catherine de'Medici, who took it over as soon as the king died, forcing Diane to accept Chaumont in return.

Now Chenonceau is one of the top attractions in France, receiving 9,000 visitors a day in summer, and is second only to Versailles. Owned by the Menier family (of chocolate fame), this is a slicker commercial operation than most châteaux and there is a separate waxworks museum

The symbolic volcano ('*chaud mont*' – hot mountain) on the walls of Chaumont castle

Above: Chenonceau on the River Cher
Right: Diane de Poitiers' garden

explaining the building's history. The château is made welcoming by large flower arrangements (plus roaring log fires in winter) and smartly dressed hostesses standing ready to answer questions.

Instead of approaching the draw-bridged entrance directly, veer left and circle the sunken garden to get the famous view of the building, with its six-arched entrance bridge across the Cher river. Inside, in the chapel, glass protects the dates scratched into the wall by Henri II's Scots Guards. In the room of Diane de Poitiers, carved 'D's and 'H's are interlinked over the fireplace, ironically beneath a replica portrait of Catherine de'Medici. The 60m-long gallery, built across the water, housed wounded soldiers in World War I; the busts of famous personages on the wall are unfortunate additions of the 19th century.

The kitchens are disappointingly bare, but the rooms above them contain several more reminders of the women of Chenonceau. The room of the Five Queens bears the coats of arms of five royal spouses, with those of Mary, Queen of Scots above the bed. On the top floor, the Louise de Lorraine Chamber recalls the widow of the assassinated Henri III, who retreated to the château and decorated her room with bone, shovel and skull motifs.

Boat trips on the Cher and child-minding facilities are attractive extras in July and August.
31km southeast of Tours on the Cher. Tel: 47 23 90 07. Open: daily. Admission charge. Son et Lumière shows early June to mid-September (tel: 47 23 94 45 for information).

Forbidding city: Chinon castle's defences are still impressive today

CHINON

'Chinon, Chinon, Chinon,
Petite ville, grand renom,
Assise sur pierre ancienne
Au haut le bois, au pied la Vienne.'

François Rabelais' verse sums up Chinon well: small town, great renown, sitting on an ancient rock, the forest above, the Vienne below. Henry II of England built the castle, at the hub of his French empire, and he died here in 1189. A decade later, his son, Richard the Lionheart died in the Old Town, at the Hôtel des États-Généraux on rue Voltaire. Today, this is one of many restored buildings on a street as atmospheric as any in France. Rabelais wrote about the Caves Painctes (sic), or Painted Caves, whose drinking club honours the 'Sacred Bottle', while the Musée Animé du Vin et de la Tonnellerie (Wine and Cooperage Museum) is aimed at modern wine-lovers. To the right, the rue Jeanne d'Arc is supposed to be the steep route she took up to the château to seek out the Dauphin, the uncrowned Charles VII (see page 92).

Château

Although a ruin, this castle still impresses, its curtain wall enclosing an area the size of four playing fields. Joan of Arc would have heard the Marie Javelle bell chiming, as it has done regularly since 1349, but only the fireplace stands in what was once the Great Hall, where she picked out the Dauphin despite his disguise. The scene is 're-created' next door in the Royal Apartments, with 15 uninspiring wax models. Similarly, the display in the Boissy Tower is a missed opportunity to

explain properly the link between the medieval monarchs of France and England. More evocative are the Mill Tower, with its superb view, and the Coudray Fort where steps lead down past side cells into the bowels of the hill.
Museum: rue de Voltaire. Tel: 47 93 25 63. Open: April to end-September, Thursday to Tuesday, 10am–noon and 2–6pm. Admission charge.
Château (tel: 47 93 13 45). Open: June to mid-September, daily 9.15am–6.45pm; rest of year, daily 9.30am–noon and 2.15–6pm (5pm in winter). Closed: December and January. Admission charge.
Chinon is 47km southwest of Tours on the D751.

FONTEVRAUD, L'ABBAYE

Empty but evocative, this once-powerful abbey is the final resting place of the early Plantagenet kings and queens of England (see page 37). Recently restored, the creamy white church is an echoing mausoleum, with just four recumbent effigies in the crypt: Henry II of England (1133–89), his sword on his left; his queen, Eleanor of Aquitaine (1122–1204), holding a bible in her hands; their son, Richard I, the Lionheart (1157–99); and their daughter-in-law, Isabelle of Angoulême (died 1246). Hers is the only wooden figure; the others are painted stone. The hearts of her husband, John I of England (1167–1216), and their son, Henry III (1207–72), are also buried in the abbey.

Another 15 years of work is needed to restore what is the largest, most complete monastic complex in France. Founded in 1099, it housed five separate communities of priests, nuns, lepers,

invalids and lay sisters – all under the management of an abbess. Protected by powerful patrons, it also provided a retreat for exiled noblewomen, such as Queen Eleanor.

Use your imagination to visualise the abbey's daily life. The cloister was not for chatting but for meditating; the chapter house held morning meetings to allocate jobs. The 16th-century murals, depicting the abbess washing the feet of the community on Good Friday, were often updated when a new abbess took over. The only room to be heated was the *chauffoir* or Salle Commune, used for writing and sewing. In the enormous refectory, nuns would only have sat on one side of the long tables, facing the wall and not each other. Cooking in the stunning Romanesque kitchens was done over one of several side hearths, lighted in pairs depending on the wind direction.

Desecrated by Huguenots in the 16th century and revolutionaries in the 1790s, Fontevraud became a gaol under Napoleon; the last prisoner only left in 1985. Today, it is a cultural centre, with concerts virtually every weekend of the year, usually held in the upper dormitory or the refectory, both noted for fine acoustics.
58km southwest of Tours, 5km south of the Loire. Tel: 41 51 73 52. Open: daily. Admission charge.

Royal family: Eleanor of Aquitaine next to her husband, Henry II of England

LADIES OF THE LOIRE

Whether peasant, mistress, seductress or queen, these ladies of the Loire made their mark on French history (see also Joan of Arc on page 92).

Agnès Sorel, royal mistress
Beautiful and intelligent, Agnès was the acknowledged favourite of King Charles VII. They spent time at Loches (see page 70) where her serene marble effigy is supported by two angels. In life, her easy-going attitude shocked many; two portraits depict her bare-breasted. While some condemned her extravagance, others praised her support for a weak king. Allegedly poisoned, she died, pregnant, in 1450.

Eleanor of Aquitaine, twice a queen
Helen of Troy caused a war of only 10-years duration; without Eleanor, the Hundred Years' War between England and France would never have happened (see page 37). Strong, beautiful and wealthy, Eleanor married Prince (later King) Louis VII of France in 1137. After the union was annulled in 1152, she married a younger man, Henry Plantagenet, Count of Anjou, bringing one-third of France as her dowry. Two years later, he was crowned Henry II of England and Eleanor was again queen. She died at Fontevraud in 1204.

relished her power and loved Chenonceau, presented to her by the king. When he died, Queen Catherine de'Medici took both the power and the château, giving Chaumont to Diane in compensation. For 10 years until her death at Blois in 1589, Catherine ruled France through her three sons, François II, Charles IX and Henri III.

Anne of Brittany, Queen of France

Brittany was an independent kingdom until it was absorbed by France at Anne's marriage to Charles VIII in 1491. Anne was then only 15; at 23, she was a widow. Moreover, the nuptial contract dictated that she marry the king's successor, Charles's cousin, Louis XII. The châteaux at Langeais, Amboise and Blois are embellished with her initial 'A', plus her symbol, the ermine. She died in 1514.

Diane de Poitiers and Catherine de'Medici; mistress versus wife

Although 20 years older than Henri II, Diane held him enthralled. She ran the court, brought up the royal children,

Escadron Volant

Catherine de'Medici's special weapon was the Flying Squad (Escadron Volant), a group of beautiful, blue-blooded Mata Haris who furthered the queen's ambitions by seducing her (male) opponents. At Chenonceau, they enlivened festivities by leaping out from behind bushes, undressed provocatively, to welcome the guests.

LE GRAND-PRESSIGNY

'We call it the capital of the Stone Age,' boasts a guide at the Prehistory Museum, located in the castle of this quiet town at the junction of the Aigronne and Claise rivers. In neolithic times, flints shaped here were exported all over Europe. Now the axes and scrapers are under glass, along with fossilised shells and sharks' teeth. The 12th-century, 35m-high castle keep dominates, while seven handsome arches in the garden are the sole reminders of a Renaissance gallery.
59km south of Tours, via the N10, D750 and D42 .

Musée Départemental de Préhistoire. Tel: 47 94 90 21. Open: daily 2–6pm (5pm in winter). Closed: December and January, also Wednesday spring and autumn. Admission charge.

The Château du Gué-Péan

GUÉ-PÉAN, CHÂTEAU DU

Gué-Péan is a typical 16th-century château – a country house masquerading as a castle. Even the defensive moat has now dried up. Situated on the edge of the Forest of Choussy, its 'hunting-lodge' description belies the luxury of its Renaissance interior. The *grand salon* has an awesome fireplace, with carved stone angels and garlands. The art collection contrasts Fragonard and Dali, Guido and Klein, Caravaggio and Carzou. Outside, three towers have the familiar pepper-pot roofs; the fourth is topped by a sterner bell-shaped dome and lantern. Had tabloid newspapers existed in the 16th century, they would have splashed news of the secret wedding here between Mary Tudor of York, sister of the English king, Henry VIII, and Charles Brandon, Duke of Suffolk. The present owner, the Marquis de Keguelin, is a hero of the World War II Resistance and a small museum honours those who fought for the movement.
Monthou-sur-Cher, 50km east of Tours, just north of the N76. Tel: 54 75 05 06. Open: daily. Admission charge.

LANGEAIS, CHÂTEAU DE

No fairy-tale château this, but rather a menacing fortress whose walls and ramparts are wedged right into the town. In 1886, M Jacques Siegfried rescued the castle, furnished it with 15th-century beds, tapestries and tables, and gave it to the state in 1904. The guiding system is disappointingly old-fashioned but there are highlights for enthusiasts.

The recently renewed drawbridge of the L-shaped castle was ordered by Louis XI in 1465 to block any attack from the Bretons. That threat evaporated when his son, Charles VIII, married Anne de Bretagne (of Brittany) here in 1491. There are reminders throughout: the initials K (for Karolus, Latin for Charles), A (for Anne), the ermine (Anne's heraldic symbol), and the *fleur de lys* of France. Some of the so-called *mille fleurs* (thousand-flower) tapestries have recognisable daffodils, pinks, violets and cowslips.

Upstairs is a reproduction of a 'noble's bed', the 13th-century precursor to the canopied four-poster, with curtains hung by ropes from the beams. Less inspiring is the re-creation of the royal wedding in the Great Hall (Room 8). Of the 15 wax mannequins, Charles and Anne are the smallest. In the group on the left, Louis d'Orléans, in black and white, studies the marriage contract. Ironically, because of its wording, he ended up becoming Anne's second husband (see page 67). Don't miss the back of the door, which is heavily carved with exotic men-at-arms.

The most atmospheric part of the castle is the 130m walk along the ramparts. Luckily the 171 machicolations

Right: the Château de Langeais
Below: waxwork version of history, as Brittany is united with France

are covered by planks, but parents should still hold on to children stretching to see the rooftop views.

Behind the château stand the ruins of the oldest surviving stone *donjon* (keep) in France, built to defend the Anjou/Touraine border in 994.
23km southwest of Tours on the N152. Tel: 47 96 72 60. Open: daily. Closed: Tuesday in winter. Admission charge.

LOCHES

Set on the Indre river, this handsome town of cobbled streets and slate-roofed, white-stone houses was once a royal residence. In 1429, Joan of Arc hurried to Loches château to persuade the Dauphin to go to Reims for his coronation (see page 92). Indecisive and glum, Charles only found cheer in Agnès Sorel, the first officially recognised royal mistress (see page 66). Despite her demure-looking white marble effigy, she knew how to show off her figure, and started a fashion at the French court of dressing in gauze, which did little to hide her shapely breasts. She also posed bare-breasted for Jean Fouquet's famous portrait of her as the Virgin Mary, a copy of which adorns the château. The square, 37m-high *donjon* (keep) built by Foulques III Nerra (see box) was used as a prison until 1926. Back in 1500, the Duke of Milan, locked up for eight years, covered the walls in military murals.
43km southeast of Tours on the N143. Château – tel: 47 59 01 32. Open: July to August, daily; rest of year, Thursday to Tuesday. Admission charge.

LOUDUN

Loudun will come as a disappointment for anyone expecting an insight into the 17th-century witch hunt that inspired Aldous Huxley's book and Ken Russell's film, *The Devils of Loudun* (1971). The ruined Tour Carrée, built by Foulques III Nerra in 1040, is the only historic building of any great merit.
72km southwest of Tours on the N147.

LE LUDE

'Wouldn't it be fun to show off some old costumes against the backdrop of the illuminated château?' That idea for the annual village fair in 1957 spawned what is one of the oldest and best of the region's *son et lumière* (sound and light) shows (see page 148). The château's 18th-century addition is sandwiched between 16th-century towers. Inside are tapestries and paintings, and the feeling is homely because the de Nicholay family still live here. Recently opened are the dimly lit underground guardroom and a passage from the earlier fortress on the site.
50km northwest of Tours, on the D306 in the Loir valley.

Time stands still in the streets of Loches

Treasure trove: Montrésor's delights have been discovered but not spoiled

Château – tel: 43 94 60 09. Open: April to end of September, daily. Admission charge. Son et lumière shows from mid-June to late August (tel: 43 94 67 27 for information).

MONTOIRE-SUR-LE-LOIR

Entertainers from a dozen countries enliven this small town during its August folk festival. Montoire's good name was tarnished on 24 October, 1940, when Adolf Hitler shook hands here with France's Marshal Pétain, who agreed to collaborate with the Nazi occupation. A fonder memory is of Pierre de Ronsard, the Renaissance poet (see page 96) who, in the late-16th century was the prior of St-Gilles, the Benedictine priory that stands on the south bank of the river, below the ruined castle. To see the Byzantine-influenced 12th- and 13th-century murals, ask for the key at M Chéreau's antique shop, in rue St-Oustrille.
45km northeast of Tours in the Loir valley.

MONTRÉSOR

The charms of the 'prettiest village in France' may pall on summer weekends when crowds of people come to see the medieval houses with their gardens running down to the Indrois river. The early 16th-century château was restored somewhat fancifully in 1849 by the Polish Count, Xavier Branicki, hence the Polish Museum of Art. Its curtain wall and towers were built by Foulques III Nerra (see box).
50km southeast Tours on the D760. Tel: 47 92 60 04. Open: April to end of October, daily. Admission charge.

FOULQUES III NERRA (987–1040)
The third Count of Anjou was a fearsome commander, a jealous husband, a greedy neighbour and an inveterate builder. His castle in Angers was one of a network stretching eastwards along the Loire valley as far as Montrésor, built to protect his conquered lands. Montbazon, Montrichard and Loudun illustrate his skill in choosing a site; the ruins at Loches and Langeais show the skill of his masons. He also founded the abbeys at Ronçeray and Beaulieu-lès-Loches, no doubt to save his soul after all that conquering and pillaging.

Novel features: Montsoreau is the setting for a popular adventure story

MONTRICHARD

Montrichard is a picturesque town of timber-framed houses clustered beneath the remains of Foulques III Nerra's *donjon* (keep) of 1010, from which there are splendid views, and occasional displays of falconry. The Romanesque church of Ste-Croix stands below the keep – it was here that a royal marriage took place in 1476, when Louis XI's daughter, Jeanne, married Louis d'Orléans. The artificial caves and quarries on the north side of the River Cher are used for growing mushrooms and maturing the sparkling wines and goat's cheeses for which the region is famous.
42km southeast of Tours on the north bank of the Cher. Donjon. Tel: 54 32 05 10.

Open: mid-June to end-August, daily; Palm Sunday to mid-June and September, weekends and public holidays only. Admission charge.

MONTSOREAU, CHÂTEAU DE

Montsoreau served as the setting for the 19th-century novel, *La Dame de Montsoreau*, though the author, Alexander Dumas, rewrote 16th-century history to make a better story. In reality, the 'hero', Bussy d'Amboise, was a cad and the Comtesse was not unfaithful to her husband: she remained faithful to him through 40 years of marriage and bore nine children. The pleasant little town, hanging over the Loire, makes a convenient base for visitors to tour the region.

Candes-St-Martin

About 1.5km southeast of Montsoreau, this surprisingly large 12th-century monastic church marks the spot where St Martin of Tours (see page 56) died on 11 November, 397. Initially he was buried here but there was considerable rivalry between the monks of Candes-St-Martin and those of Tours over the possession of the saint's remains. In the end, the monks of Tours decided to 'kidnap' the saint. As they rowed his body upstream to Tours, the bare trees along the banks are supposed to have bloomed miraculously, even though it was November. The phrase 'St Martin's summer', meaning a freak spell of fine weather, was used by both the French and the English in the old days but has now died out.

Château – tel: 41 51 70 25. Open: daily (but closed Tuesday from mid-December to late February). Admission charge.

56km southwest of Tours on the south bank of the Loire, 11km from Saumur.

PLESSIS-LÈS-TOURS, CHÂTEAU DE

Louis XI would be scandalised to see the degree to which suburban bungalows have encroached upon his château, romantically (but inaccurately) described in Sir Walter Scott's novel *Quentin Durward* (1823). Only the south wing survives of the old manor house modernised by the king from 1461. Although the moat and drawbridge hark back to defensive needs, the château was domestic in appearance and its design, with decorative patterns of bricks contrasting with stone, established a new fashion.

Mad about hunting, the king had a game park near by stocked with exotic animals, and he spent his last six years here. Paranoid about his safety and (falsely) believing himself to be suffering from leprosy, he prowled about the kitchens hoping to overhear plots on his life; terrified of death he lavished money on religious orders. He died in 1483, in an austere-looking room whose plain stone fireplace and brick walls are only somewhat offset by the fine 'pleated' effect of the wood panelling. The building also houses the Tours Museum of Ceramics and Silk.

3km from Tours, in the western suburb of La Riche. Tel: 47 37 22 80. Open: Wednesday to Tuesday 10am–noon and 2–6pm (to 5pm from October to end of March). Admission charge.

PRIEURÉ DE ST-COSMÉ

The nearby railway line and main road disturb the peace that Pierre de Ronsard, the 'Prince of Poets', would have enjoyed when he was put in charge of this priory in 1565. Then, he worked in his garden, dallied with his 15-year-old mistress (to the scandal of the older monks) and entertained pilgrims on their way south to Santiago de Compostela. He also put off until another day the task of finishing the *Françiade*, an epic poem commissioned by his patron, Charles IX. Today, the gardens are neat and his tomb is shaded by roses. Gregorian chant (played over loudspeakers) drowns out the sound of creaking floorboards in the 12th-century monk's refectory where an elaborate lectern survives. The prior's lodge, Ronsard's plain stone home, is now a museum.

3km from Tours, in the western suburb of La Riche. Tel: 47 37 32 70. Open: July and August, daily; rest of year, Thursday to Tuesday. Admission charge.

'Troglodyte: a cave-dweller, especially in prehistoric Western Europe.' What the dictionary doesn't say is that cave-dwellers still exist in the Loire Valley, not living in primitive burrows but in homes with modern conveniences. The practical French have many uses for caves and quarries: you can even rent a *troglogîte* for a self-catering holiday underground. The best example of these homes is to be seen alongside the D947 between Montsoreau and Saumur.

Tuffe
The houses and châteaux of the Loire Valley are mainly quarried out of white *tuffe* (tufa), a limestone that cuts easily and hardens on contact with air. Millions of cubic metres have been extracted from the cliffs that line the

TROGLODYTES

Chez moi: yesterday's peasant abodes are today's museums and restaurants

Loire, Cher, Indre, Loir and Vienne rivers. The resulting galleries are used to store sparkling wines that need to be turned gently over many months, and also for growing mushrooms, which thrive in the darkness and constant temperature.

Crushed seashells

Falun (oolitic limestone), formed from seashells crushed millions of years ago, is slightly different from tufa. Excavated on farmland south of the Loire, it was once converted to lime for agricultural purposes. Unlike caverns in cliffs, these quarries are hard to spot below the fields of sunflowers but these, too, contrive to be used for homes and storage, with extra galleries dug to create corridors and chambers.

Some are converted into popular, if touristy, restaurants serving hot *fouaces* (bread) baked in wood-fired ovens. One is a museum reflecting everyday life a century ago: another is used for making *pommes tapées* (dried apples); a third is a silkworm farm (see page 172–3); and a fourth is a zoo, complete with flamingos and cheetahs.

Cardinal points: the perfect symmetry of Richelieu's town planning

RICHELIEU

As the name suggests, this town was created in 1651 by the statesman, Cardinal Richelieu, as a model example of town planning. Richelieu's magnificent palace was dismantled after the Revolution, but the rectilinear town, with its three triumphal-arched entrances, has survived. Twenty-eight identical houses, with individual carriage entrances, line the Grande-Rue; the lower ranks lived behind.

Champigny-sur-Veude

Jealous of the magnificence of the Bourbon-Montpensier château (6km north of Richelieu), Cardinal Richelieu bought it, then destroyed it. Luckily, the 16th-century Chapelle St-Louis remains; the colours of the stained glass, particularly the blues, are still intense 400 years on.

Town hall museum – tel: 47 58 13 62. Open: daily in July and August. Closed: Tuesday and weekends, September to June. Park open: mid-June to mid-September, daily. Admission charge. Chapelle St-Louis – tel: 47 95 71 46.

Open: April to early October, daily. Admission charge.

Richelieu is 62km southwest of Tours on the D757.

SACHÉ, CHÂTEAU DE

Honoré de Balzac (1799–1850) wrote a good number of his 85 novels while staying in this 16th-century château, now furnished as it was in his lifetime. Fans of the 19th-century novelist (see page 96) come to see his rather plain room in the east wing, with its view of the Indre river and its desk with quill pen and inkwell. He wrote solidly from 5am to 5pm; then read out what he had written to his hosts, the Margonne family. Another local resident, Alexander Calder (1898–1976), famous for his mobiles, lived here for the last 20 years of his life. One of his works remains on the village square.

Saché is 18km southwest of Tours on the Indre river.

Château – tel: 47 26 86 50. Open: daily, July and August; rest of year, Thursday to Tuesday. Closed: Wednesdays in the low season and all December. Admission charge.

STE-MAURE-DE-TOURAINE

The annual cheese fair in June celebrates *le chèvre de Ste-Maure*, the local goat's cheese identified by the straw running through it. The *fermier* (farm-made) versions are better than the industrial, paper-wrapped *laitier* product.
37km southwest of Tours on the N10.

SEUILLY

Rabelais, the burlesque writer, would have laughed to hear experts argue over 'when' and 'where' he was born. Between 1483 and 1494? At 15 rue de la Lamproie in Chinon? Or at the family farm in La Devinière? Or even in a field, like his legendary hero, Gargantua? La Devinière is now a literary shrine with a small museum of Rabelaisian memorabilia.
52km southwest of Tours. Tel: 47 95 91 18. Open: May to end-September, daily; rest of year, Thursday to Tuesday. Admission charge.

TRÔO

A sleepy artists' colony on the Loir river, Trôo is a showcase for troglodyte homes, many with pretty gardens and terraces (see page 85). Climb the steep winding paths and steps to Le Puits qui parle, the 45m-deep 'Talking Well', renowned for its echo. Pilgrims to St Martin's church sought a cure for stomach trouble.

Trôo is 54km north of Tours in the Loir Valley.

La Possonnière

This elegant, Renaissance-influenced country mansion (situated 8km southwest of Trôo) is now a shrine to the poet Pierre de Ronsard (see page 96) who was born here in 1524. Look for the burning roses (*roses ardentes*) on the fireplace in the dining-room, a visual pun (or rebus) on Ronsard's name.
La Possoniére – tel: 54 72 40 05. Open: guided tours at 3pm and 5pm daily in July and August, weekends and public holidays during the rest of the year. Admission charge.

Contemporary artists enjoy the peace of Trôo on Le Loir

USSÉ, CHÂTEAU D'

Who needs Walt Disney's version of Sleeping Beauty's castle when you can see the real thing? Charles Perrault, the 17th-century fairy-tale author, had this château in mind when he wrote *La Belle au bois dormant* (*The Beauty of the Sleeping Wood*, on which *Sleeping Beauty* is based). Of the castle's 10 tableaux depicting the story, the spooky witch in her cave is the best. These tableaux, plus the display of costumes (changed every year to focus on a different century) make this castle more interesting than many for children, while the recently restored Chambre du Roi, the 15th-century ebony-and-ivory-inlaid Italian cabinet or the tapestries in the long gallery will appeal to the grown-ups. In the park is a small 16th-century chapel; its Aubusson tapestries have been stolen, but the Renaissance stall and door carvings remain.

The 'sleeping wood' of Perrault's story, the dense forest of Chinon, stands right behind, offsetting the chimneys,

Above: Ussé is popular with children
Left: the château tapestries are Flemish

gables, towers and turrets, which were added over the centuries as successive owners 'improved' the building. With the River Indre below, the overall look is charmingly 'romantic'.

40km southwest of Tours, just south of the Loire. Tel: 47 95 54 05. Open: daily. Admission charge.

Cabbages and kings: Villandry has the world's most elegant vegetable garden

VILLANDRY, CHÂTEAU DE

Villandry is famous for its gardens, which are a 'must-see', even for those who hate gardening. The geometric patterns of the beds and borders look like the doodles of a mathematician, complete with allegorical references to decipher. Don't miss the kitchen garden, where the vegetables are grown and prized as much for their ornamental value as for consumption. Pink-hearted cabbages were cultivated at Villandry long before they were seen in trendy garden centres.

The gardens, like the château, reflect the Italian influence on 16th-century France. Villandry claims to be the last of the great Renaissance châteaux to be built on the Loire (although it is actually on the south bank of the Cher river). Constructed in 1536 by Jean le Breton, Secretary of State to François I, it was saved in 1906 by Dr Joachim de Carvallo, who restored the castle as well as the gardens. An ardent conservationist, he also founded the Historic Houses Association of France. His Spanish heritage is reflected in the family collection of 17th- and 18th-century paintings, which include works by Goya and Velázquez, and a fine *Assumption* by Murillo.

15km west of Tours on the D7, 10km from Azay-le-Rideau. Tel: 47 50 02 09. Gardens open: daily. Château open: mid-March to mid-November. Admission charge.

VOUVRAY

Vouvray means wine: it's as simple as that. This village on the Loire, along with its neighbours, Rochecorbon and Parçay-Meslay, produce fine white wines, still and sparkling, dry, medium and sweet. The vines grow on the plateau above; the bottles fill endless galleries in the cliffs below. Visit these and taste the wines at well-known makers such as Marc Brédif where a circular tasting room has been hollowed out, deep within the rock.

10km east of Tours on the north bank of the Loire.

Old Tours

The Quartier Plumereau, the city's old quarter, is full of cafés, students and delightfully carved *hôtels* (mansions) of timber and stone, now restored thanks to a 35-year renovation programme. *Allow 1 hour.*

Start in place du Grand Marché by the tourist information board. Walk north up rue Bretonneau.

1 RUE BRETONNEAU

The Hôtel des Seigneurs d'Ussé, at No 22, is 15th-century Gothic, though it now houses a Moroccan restaurant. Opposite, the Hôtel Poulet-Grellay recalls the Renaissance, but was built in the 19th century. A plaque on No 35 records the birthplace of the French Communist Party at the Congress of Tours in 1920.

Turn right on to rue des Cerisiers.

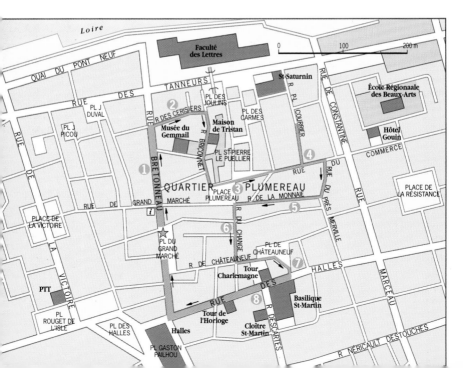

2 RUE DES CERISIERS

Number 7 was a 19th-century ladies' academy where the sisters of the famous novelist, Honoré de Balzac, were educated. Turning right on to rue Briçonnet, the handsome Hôtel des Cordeliers, at No 16, is also known as Tristan's House. Try spotting the frog among the carvings above the windows; you will need binoculars to see the detail of the statue at the pinnacle of the Flemish-style gable. Built by Pierre Dupui in 1498, a witty anagram of his name in the interior courtyard reads 'Prie Dieu Pur'.
Continue to place Plumereau.

3 PLACE PLUMEREAU

The heart of Old Tours bustles with as many locals as tourists, attracted by the art galleries, boutiques and cafés. Spend a few moments taking in the mixture of architectural styles, as 15th-century timber-frame buildings alternate with later stone buildings.
Turn left (east) along rue du Commerce.

4 RUE DU COMMERCE

Here, garish restaurants clash with handsome houses, particularly Nos 106–110, with their tall 18th-century windows and balconies. Dip left into rue Paul-Louis Courier. Finely carved heads mark No 17, where the Florentine sculptor, Giovanni Giusti (Jean Juste) lived from 1504. Number 15 is the site of the house where Joan of Arc stayed in 1429. The Hôtel Binet, No 10, is an outstanding 15th-century mansion with a wooden gallery above the inner courtyard, reached by spiral staircases.
Return to rue du Commerce; turn left, then right on rue du Président Merville (past the Museum of Natural History), then right again on to rue de la Monnaie.

5 RUE DE LA MONNAIE

The Hôtel de la Monnaie, at No 7, was a mint, producing *sols, deniers* and golden *louis* coins from the 13th century until it closed in 1772.
Continue towards place Plumereau. Turn left on to the rue du Change.

6 RUE DU CHANGE

On the corner is a wonderful 15th-century house decorated with a carving of the Nativity. At the bottom of the street is the tall, ivy-clad tower of the Briçonnet-Berthelot house, home of the first mayor of Tours, Jean Briçonnet.
Turn left on to place de Châteauneuf.

7 PLACE DE CHÂTEAUNEUF

The Logis des Ducs de Touraine was the private mansion of the Dukes of Touraine back in the 15th and 16th centuries.
Bear right, on to rue des Halles.

8 RUE DES HALLES

This street cuts right through the site of the Basilica of St-Martin, pulled down 200 years ago. All that remains are the Tour Charlemagne on the right and, opposite, the tomb of St-Martin in the crypt of the 19th-century basilica, plus the Tour de l'Horloge (clock tower) further down the street.
Continue past the clock tower and turn right to return to place du Grand Marché.

The Indre

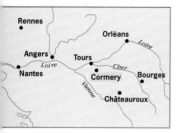

A tranquil river, with picnic sites around every
bend in the adjacent road, the Indre has long been
at the crossroads of history. This drive goes from
Cormery to Buzançais, through pretty countryside
with plenty of farms but few tourists. *Allow half a
day for the 75km journey, longer if you decide to
stop and explore.*

Start in Cormery.

1 CORMERY

The 50m-high tower of St-Paul is just one indication of the
grandeur of the Benedictine monastery founded here in 791.
Remnants of the Romanesque cloisters,
refectory and chapel still stand in the
town. Today, Cormery is more renowned
for its macaroons.
Take the D17 to Chambourg.

2 CHAMBOURG-SUR-INDRE

The road on the north bank is quiet, with
the sleepy villages of Courçay, Reignac
and Azay.
*At Chambourg, cross the bridges to the south
bank of the Indre, following the D94 and
then the D25 to Beaulieu-les-Loches.*

3 BEAULIEU-LES-LOCHES

This looks like an extension of Loches on
the opposite bank, but Beaulieu's
religious community constantly battled
for power with the royal court across the
river. Foulques III Nerra, the 11th-
century warlord, founded the abbey (now
in ruins) where he was later buried.
*Staying on the north side of the Indre, follow
the D92, then the D28, then cross the bridge
into Châtillon.*

4 CHÂTILLON-SUR-INDRE

Built on a spur of chalk overlooking the
river and its peaceful fields, this medieval

Well-beaten: French soldiers tunnelled to victory at Palluau-sur-Indre

village of narrow stone streets is full of history. The tourist office has a useful pamphlet mapping out a walk past the 16th-century Maison Henri III, with its fine entrance, and the market square, with its panoramic view. The 12th-century church has a portal with carvings of Adam and Eve being chased from Eden, plus dancing donkeys, beasts and mythical creatures. The 13th-century château boasts a massive keep, a legacy of Henry II of England.
Cross the bridge to the north bank of the Indre again and pick up the D28 to Palluau.

5 PALLUAU-SUR-INDRE

This village has a special place in Canadian history since Louis de Buade (1620–98), Count of Frontenac and owner of the impressive castle, was made governor of the French possessions in North America in 1672. He took with him Jean-Baptiste Franquelin, another local, who mapped out the territory of Nouvelle-France (New France), which then extended from Canada to the Gulf of Mexico. The Philippe-Auguste Tower commemorates the French king who besieged and defeated Richard the Lionheart here in 1188. English survival depended on a well 108m deep, so when the French tunnelled into the hillside they cut the well-rope. With no water supply, the English were forced to surrender.
Leave Palluau on the D15e; then take the D64 to Buzançais.

6 BUZANÇAIS

This quiet market town today, known for its porcelain, has been fought over many times and, as recently as 1846, the peasants revolted against a tax on wheat.
Return to the Loire via the fast but busy N143, along the south bank of the Indre.

Le Loir

Not to be confused with La Loire, this smaller river wanders past small towns and villages plus vineyards and fields of sunflowers. The poet Pierre de Ronsard (1524–1585) was born and lived on its banks. The route follows a 40km-stretch between Château-du-Loir and Lavardin. *Allow at least half a day.*

1 CHÂTEAU-DU-LOIR
The keep that gave its name to the village is now a ruin, but the 13th-century church of St-Guingalois, where Ronsard once worshipped, contains fine sculpture in wood and terracotta.
Take the N138 to Coëmont and turn left on the D64. The road, squeezed between the limestone cliff and the railway line, follows the north bank.

2 VOUVRAY-SUR-LOIR
Many wine cellars are open to the public and wine lovers should contact the town hall (tel: 43 44 14 15) for details of the tastings that take place on Fridays in summer in the municipal cellars, dug out of the cliffs.
Follow the D64 towards Chahaignes. Just after Le Port Gautier, turn right for Marçon, crossing the railway and the narrow bridge.

3 MARÇON
The large lake on the left is part of a leisure park offering riding, fishing, sailing and tennis. Marçon itself has a fine, oblong square lined with lime trees. Old houses are being restored and shops sell the renowned local wine.

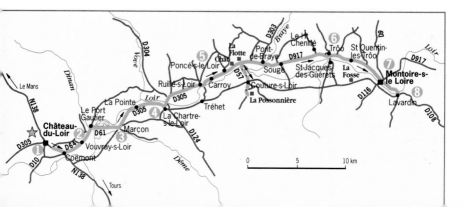

La Chartre: a popular halt for fans of good food and motor-racing

Turn left on the D305 towards La Chartre. The river is now on your left.

4 LA CHARTRE-SUR-LE-LOIR
This is a classic small French town, with a main square ringed by tempting food and wine shops. The ivy-clad Hôtel de France attracts motor-racing teams for the Le Mans 24-hour race and fans come to see the signed photos in the bar.
Leave by one of the three bridges over the Loir, staying on the D305 for Ruillé and passing through the Jasnières and Côteaux du Loir vineyards where several growers offer dégustations (tastings).

5 PONCÉ-SUR-LE-LOIR
Stop here to see the crafts centre housed in the 18th-century buildings of the former Paillard paper mill. Watch artisans at work, or try throwing a pot on a wheel. The 16th-century château opposite has a remarkable staircase whose ceiling is carved with allegorical subjects, and a dovecot that once housed 1,800 pigeons.
Continue on D305. An optional detour is

south on the D57 to La Possonnière, Ronsard's birthplace (see page 77). Otherwise continue through Pont-de-Braye to Trôo.

6 TRÔO
The homes of Trôo's troglodyte community can be visited daily between mid-July and mid-August (see page 77). *Follow the D917 to Montoire. Garden lovers might detour to the right to see the botanical gardens at La Fosse.*

7 MONTOIRE-SUR-LE-LOIR
Visit the chapel and prior's lodging where Ronsard spent his last years (see page 71). The chapel has outstanding Romanesque frescos.
Continue on the D917 to Lavardin.

8 LAVARDIN
One of France's most atmospheric villages, Lavardin is dominated by its ruined 12th-century castle. The church of St-Genest has impressive 13th-century frescos of the *Passion* and *Christ in Majesty.*

East Central Loire

*T*he Centre-Val-de-Loire administrative region has Orléans as its capital, the city relieved by Joan of Arc in 1429, an event still celebrated annually with grand parades in May. For centuries before that, Orléans had been a major city under the Capet dynasty. Blois, however, claims to have been the capital of France under King Louis XII, who was born in the city in 1462. Today, it is one of the Loire's most attractive cities, with an extensive pedestrian area in the old quarter, a grand town hall in the former Bishop's Palace and a château that looks like a mini-city in its own right.

Châteaux

The best-known château in this region, is Chambord, the world's largest hunting lodge, with its ingenious double staircase. Other, less famous, castles have developed themes to attract visitors: Chamerolles concentrates on perfume, while La Ferté-St-Aubin offers cookery demonstrations. At Sully, a 20-year project is under way to restore the home of its 17th-century Duke, one of France's most able ministers. Talcy was the home of two women, generations apart, who inspired great poetry, while the portrait gallery of Beauregard is a 'who's who' of France in the 14th to 17th centuries. Cheverny, dedicated to hunting, is very much a family home.

Churches and abbeys

Great ecclesiastical buildings abound, from the grandeur of Orléans cathedral to the little-visited Germigny-des-Prés, modestly hiding a 1,200-year-old apsidal mosaic. La Trinité Church in Vendôme is a masterpiece of Flamboyant Gothic and the church at Cléry-St-André has the skulls of a French king and queen. Finally, pay tribute to St Benedict, founder of western monasticism, whose remains are buried at St-Benoît-sur-Loire.

Royal Blois: a former capital of France with a fine château, museums, and cathedral

EAST CENTRAL LOIRE

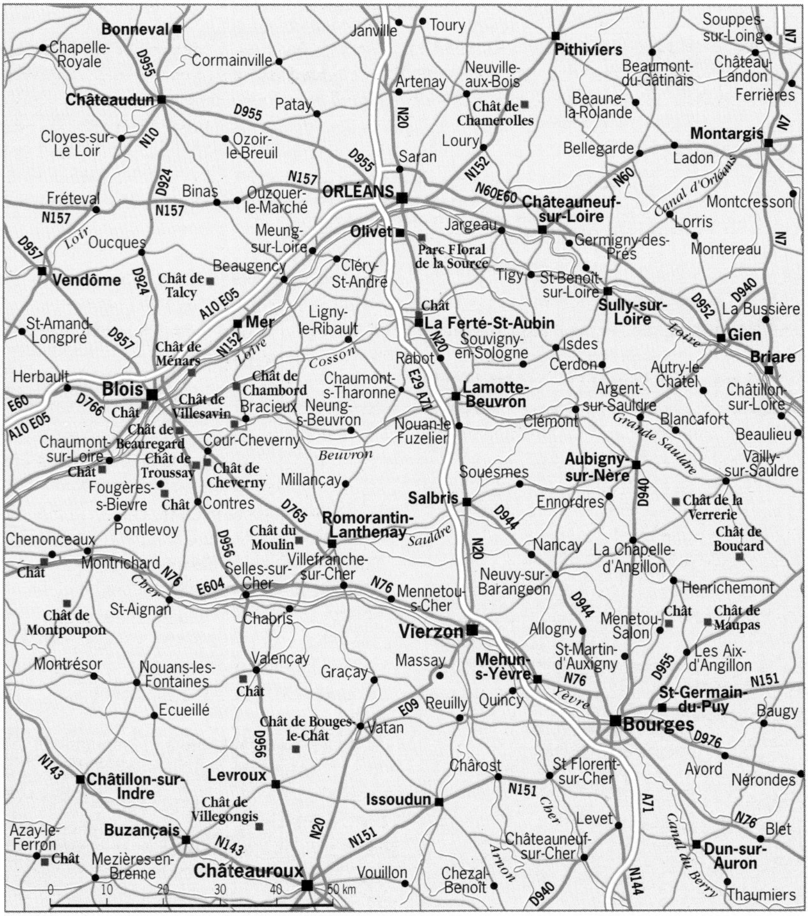
Bonneval
Janville
Toury
Chapelle-Royale
Cormainville
Pithiviers
Souppes-sur-Loing
Beaumont-du-Gâtinais
Château-Landon
Ferrières
Neuville-aux-Bois
Artenay
Châteaudun
Patay
Chât de Chamerolles
Beaune-la-Rolande
Cloyes-sur-Le Loir
Ozoir-le-Breuil
Loury
Bellegarde
Montargis
Ladon
Saran
Fréteval
Binas
Ouzouer-le-Marché
ORLÉANS
Châteauneuf-sur-Loire
Canal d'Orléans
Montcresson
Lorris
Oucques
Meung-sur-Loire
Olivet
Jargeau
Germigny-des-Prés
Montereau
Parc Floral de la Source
Vendôme
Beaugency
Cléry-St-André
Tigy
St-Benoît-sur-Loire
Chât de Talcy
Chât
La Ferté-St-Aubin
Sully-sur-Loire
La Bussière
Gien
St-Amand-Longpré
Mer
Ligny-le-Ribault
Souvigny-en-Sologne
Isdes
Briare
Chât de Ménars
Rabot
Cerdon
Cosson
Herbault
Blois
Chât de Chambord
Chaumont-s-Tharonne
Lamotte-Beuvron
Argent-sur-Sauldre
Autry-le-Châtel
Châtillon-sur-Loire
Chât
Chât de Villesavin
Bracieux
Neung-s-Beuvron
Clémont
Blancafort
Grande Sauldre
Chât de Beauregard
Nouan-le-Fuzelier
Beaulieu
Chaumont-sur-Loire
Cour-Cheverny
Beuvron
Vailly-sur-Sauldre
Chât
Chât de Troussay
Chât de Cheverny
Millançay
Souesmes
Aubigny-sur-Nère
Fougères-s-Bievre
Chât
Contres
Salbris
Ennordres
Chât de la Verrerie
Pontlevoy
Romorantin-Lanthenay
Chât de Boucard
Chenonceaux
Chât du Moulin
Sauldre
Nancay
La Chapelle-d'Angillon
Chât
Montrichard
Villefranche-sur-Cher
Selles-sur-Cher
Neuvy-sur-Barangeon
Cher
St-Aignan
Mennetou-s-Cher
Henrichemont
Chât de Montpoupon
Chabris
Vierzon
Allogny
Menetou-Salon
Chât
Chât de Maupas
Valençay
Massay
Mehun-s-Yèvre
St-Martin-d'Auxigny
Les Aix-d'Angillon
Montrésor
Nouans-les-Fontaines
Graçay
Chât
Quincy
Yèvre
St-Germain-du-Puy
Baugy
Ecueillé
Reuilly
Bourges
Chât de Bouges-le-Château
Vatan
Avord
Châtillon-sur-Indre
Levroux
Chârost
St Florent-sur-Cher
Nérondes
Chât de Villegongis
Issoudun
Levet
Cher
Canal du Berry
Blet
Azay-le-Ferron
Buzançais
Châteauneuf-sur-Cher
Dun-sur-Auron
Chât
Mezières-en-Brenne
Châteauroux
Vouillon
Chezal-Benoît
Arnon
Thaumiers
Loire
Loir
0 10 20 30 40 50 km

Food and wine

The region has produced such chefs as the great Marie-Antoine Carême, 19th-century author of *La Cuisine française*, who worked his magic in the kitchens at Valençay, and the Tatin sisters who transformed disaster into triumph by rescuing an apple pie that had 'gone wrong' and so inventing the tarte Tatin. Among wines, those of Quincy and Reuilly should be better known than they are, and it is a short step to Sancerre, with its characteristically dry white wines.

Orléans

Orléans is famous for La Pucelle d'Orléans, the Maid of Orléans, Joan of Arc. Not surprisingly, her story has sparked a local mini-industry, culminating in the annual May re-enactment of her entrance into the besieged city in 1429.

Orléans has always been important as a trading post. Goods from as far south as the Massif Central, and from as far west as Nantes, were brought here by water, then transferred to carts for the onward journey to Paris. The city's strategic location, and its commerce, have made it a prize fought over in wars throughout French history.

Above: The ancient choir stalls
Facing page: Crowning glory – tiaras of stone top the towers of Ste-Croix Cathedral

During the 16th-century Wars of Religion, the cathedral was one of the casualties. At the end of the 19th century, following bombardment during the Franco-Prussian War of 1870–71, the Parisian-style boulevard, the rue de la République, was built. Unfortunately, the post-World War II reconstruction is not so handsome.

Although not the largest city in the Centre-Val-du-Loire, Orléans is the regional capital. It had an ancient university, whose students included Rabelais and Jean Calvin, founder of Calvinism, but this closed in 1793 when enrolment was down to only one student. The modern university is located 8km away, at Orléans-la-Source. This, plus the fact that Orléans is only 130km from Paris, close enough for thousands to commute daily on the TGV, means that the city lacks the liveliness of, say Tours. Locals admit that 'it is a ghost town after 9pm' and has only a limited choice of hotels.

Having said that, the city has some delightful old buildings and streets. The area around the medieval rue de Bourgogne is criss-crossed by *venelles* (alleys), while the rue d'Escures is lined with decorated 16th- and 17th-century mansions, most now occupied by banks. Tucked away in the rue de Notre-Dame

Left: Orléans' neo-Gothic cathedral

Cathedral of Ste-Croix

Most cathedrals of the Loire form part of an atmospheric old quarter. This one stands on an open square, passed by traffic and skateboarders who whizz along the broad terraces. Begun in 1287, it was largely destroyed by Protestants in 1568 (see page 59) but Henri IV repaid the loyalty of the town by promising to repair the damage. Rebuilding, in neo-Gothic style, took more than 250 years. Blue sky can be seen through the filigree stonework that crowns the two towers. Inside, ten stained-glass windows tell Joan of Arc's story, from her first vision of St Michael, clad in golden armour, to her death at the stake. On the north side is the tomb of Cardinal Touchet, Bishop of Orléans, whose kneeling effigy looks up to Joan's statue. His efforts led to her canonisation in 1920.

Hôtel Cabu

Heavily restored, this Renaissance mansion houses the Historical Museum. Pride of place is given to a horde of Gallo-Roman bronzes, including sculptures of a horse and a wild boar, found near by at Neuvy-en-Sullias in 1861. Upstairs are fine medieval sculptures and sections devoted to local ceramics, clocks, goldwork and folklore. *place Abbé Desnoyers. Tel: 38 53 39 22. Open: Wednesday to Monday. Admission charge, except Sunday morning and Wednesday.*

Hôtel Groslot

The 16th-century Hôtel Groslot once served as the town hall. It still houses municipal offices, but visitors are allowed to see several rooms, entering via the left-hand staircase. Back in 1560, when

de la Recouvrance, is the Hôtel Toutin, where King François I rendezvoused with his mistress; his smirking statue sits in the courtyard. The spacious place du Martroi, with its mounted statue of Joan of Arc, is faced by the elegant 18th-century Chancellerie. In the southeast of the old city, an exciting long-term project aims to revitalise the Quartier Dessaux area, once dominated by its vinegar and mustard factories. Most characteristic of all, perhaps, is the approach to the cathedral along a broad street named, of course, rue Jeanne d'Arc.

François II and his wife, Mary, Queen of Scots, stayed here, the 17-year old monarch suddenly fell ill. His doctors recommended drilling a hole in the king's head to relieve his pain, but his mother, Catherine de'Medici, refused to allow this and the king died. A large canvas depicting the death scene hangs in the ornate King's Room, where marriages now take place.
place de l'Etape. Tel: 38 42 27 48 or 38 42 22 30. Open: daily; closed Saturday morning. Free.

Musée des Beaux-Arts

The strength of this collection is the work of 16th- and 17th-century artists of the Italian, French and Dutch schools, including paintings by Matteo di Giovanni, Tintoretto and Ruysdaal. Several paintings rescued from Cardinal Richelieu's palace have a room to themselves. In the basement, a small modern collection surrounds a room dedicated to Max Jacob, the poet and artist who lived near by at St-Benoît-sur-Loire. A small work called *Visions of War* (1940) is a chilling premonition of his own death in a Nazi concentration camp.
rue Paul-Belmondo, place Ste-Croix. Tel: 38 53 39 22. Open: see Hôtel Cabu. Admission charge, except Sunday morning and Wednesday.

LES FÊTES DE JEANNE D'ARC
For over 500 years, this festival, held between 29 April and 8 May, has celebrated Joan 'for her glory, not, as in Rouen, for her martyrdom'. A schoolgirl is chosen to play the role of *La Pucelle*. Mounted on a horse and dressed in armour, she enters the city through a (temporarily) reconstructed Burgundy Gate. Over the next nine days, there are parades through the city, cathedral services, civic ceremonies and fireworks.

LA MAISON DE JEANNE D'ARC
This is a replica of the home of Jacques Boucher, with whom Joan stayed on 29 April, 1429. Less a museum, more a '*maison des souvenirs*' (house of memories), its displays explain the sequence of events leading to the raising of the siege of Orléans. A short 'mini *son et lumière*', using a model of the city, is offered in several languages.
3 place de Gaulle (tel: 38 52 99 89 or 38 42 25 45). Open: May to end-October, 10am–noon and 2–6pm; rest of year 2–6pm. Closed: Monday. Admission charge.

Roman bronze in the Hôtel Cabu

THE MAID OF ORLEANS (1412–31)

Born in eastern France, Joan of Arc was an illiterate peasant who, as a child, saw 'angels' exhorting her to free her country from the English. In late winter 1429, aged just 17, she set off with a band of six soldiers to see the Dauphin at Chinon, a journey that involved walking for 600km through dangerous territory.

AN INDICISIVE KING

When he heard of her mission, the 26-year-old monarch put on ordinary clothes and mingled with his courtiers to test Joan's powers: she recognised him at once. She persuaded him to march upon Orléans, gathering an army as he went, and halting at Blois for the bishop's blessing.

THE SIEGE OF ORLÉANS

Under siege for six months, Orléans was the last stronghold of the French against the English, who had conquered much of the Loire Valley. Joan wanted to attack the English at once, but she was thwarted by the military leaders, so she entered the city by herself, via the eastern Burgundy Gate. The welcome was huge and, on 6 May, she led an impromptu attack against the English, forcing them to retreat.

The next day, the French captured Les Tourelles, the fortress guarding the city's main bridge (now the Pont Georges V). Legend says that Joan placed a scaling ladder against the walls and, although wounded by a crossbow bolt, shrugged off the injury

and resumed the battle. The next morning, a confident French army faced the English, who took one look and retreated. Orléans was free.

FROM BETRAYAL TO BEATIFICATION

Next, Joan led the French army to drive the enemy from the Loire Valley and watched while Charles VII was crowned at Reims on 17 July, 1429. Yet the king offered no help when she was betrayed by the Burgundians, tried by French bishops and burnt at the stake by the English. That was in 1431. Not until 1920 was she canonised and declared the patron saint of France.

BEAUGENCY

Much restored, this is now one of the most attractive towns in the region. Locals are nicknamed *les chats* (the cats) because the ancient bridge was supposedly built by the devil in exchange for the soul of the first creature to cross it – crafty locals ensured that this was a cat. The 'Devil's Bridge' is the only river crossing for many kilometres up or

Rich and famous: Beauregard's unique gallery boasts 363 portraits

downstream, and its strategic importance is emphasised by the still-impressive Tour de César, the ruined 11th-century keep, built to protect the bridge. Across the road is the fine Romanesque abbey church of Notre-Dame, while the Château Dunois, containing a museum of local life (Musée Régional de l'Orleanais), stands to the north.
29km southwest of Orléans.Château, 2 place Dunois. Tel: 38 44 55 23 or 38 44 92 73. Open: Wednesday to Monday. Admission charge.

BEAUREGARD, CHÂTEAU DE
Confused by French history of the 14th to 17th centuries? Head for Beauregard's remarkable portrait gallery with its painted beams, Delft floor tiles, painted panelling and 363 faces ranged in three tiers along the walls. All of the Valois and early Bourbon kings are here, plus the VIPs of their time. Study the face of the Duc de Guise, the Catholic leader during the Wars of Religion, who stares coldly and shrewdly straight back. The Cabinet des Grelots is a delightful study, covered in paintings and carvings of *grelots* (bells) from the coat of arms of the 16th-century owner, Jean du Thiers, who turned an old hunting lodge into this elegant château on the Beuvron river.
65km southwest of Orléans, 6km south of Blois. Tel: 54 70 40 05 or 47 47 05 41. Open: daily. Closed: Wednesday from October to Easter, and all January. Admission charge.

BLOIS

Once the capital of France and famous for its château, Blois is a thoroughly likeable town, run for many years by Jack Lang, the charismatic mayor who went on to become the French Minister of Culture. Stop at the tourist office in the grounds of the château to pick up tour leaflets and wear comfortable shoes for walking on the cobbles and climbing the hills and stone steps, especially in the medieval Puits-Châtel quarter, with its mixture of half-timbered and stone mansions.

Château

The château, fascinating for its architecture and for its tales of love and intrigue, also houses four museums. The oldest room is the 13th-century Salle des Etats (Hall of States), simply designed but heavily decorated. Two centuries later, the St-Calais chapel was built after poet-duke Charles d'Orléans returned from 25 years in the Tower of London. His son, Louis, unexpectedly became King Louis XII in 1498. His additions include the brick-and-stone east wing and the charming pavilion in the gardens (now the tourist office). Next came François I, whose wing has an elaborate, semi-open staircase facing the courtyard and, facing the town, the extraordinary Façade des Loges, whose tiers of galleries look like theatre boxes.

Blois is also known for the assassination in 1598 of the Duc de Guise, the ultra-Catholic, ultra-powerful rival of Henri III during the Wars of Religion (see page 59). The deed was done in the Chambre du Roi (King's Room), with Henri supposedly listening behind the small door. Within a year Henri himself had been murdered. The study of his mother, Catherine

de'Medici, is heavily decorated; some of the 200 panels hide secret drawers and cupboards, allegedly for storing her poisons.

The complex has museums of archaeology and local history, sculpture, painting and also of locks and keys. Must-sees are the romanticised 18th-century rendition of the Duc de Guise's murder in the art collection and the gallery devoted to mechanical wizard, inventor and magician, Jean-Eugène Robert-Houdin. Children are fascinated, particularly by his clocks. The *son et lumière* in summer is one of the Loire Valley's best.

Tel: 54 78 06 62. Open: mid-March to November, daily. Son et lumière shows from June to September (tel: 54 78 06 62 for details). Admission charge.

59km southwest of Orléans on the north bank of the Loire.

CHAMBORD

Chambord is the largest of all the Loire châteaux. Some 1,800 men worked on the decoration of the 440 rooms, putting in 365 fireplaces and 83 staircases. Marshes were drained and the Cosson river re-routed. Despite all this, there was no proper kitchen and only limited toilets, for this was no more than a hunting lodge and a stage for displaying the wealth of François I. When Charles V of Spain visited in 1539, he was suitably stunned by the gilded roof, fine furniture and tapestries, all brought in just for his visit.

Today the interior is disappointingly empty, except for the château's signature feature, the double-helix staircase where visitors walk up and down in sight of one another, yet never meeting. The stone masons must have

Above: Chambord, royal hunting lodge
Right: the ingenious spiral staircases

tired of carving hundreds of fire-breathing salamanders and letter 'F's, the emblems of the king that decorate the palace, particularly in the *studiolo*, or little study. Otherwise, the audio-visual and model displays do their best to explain a grandeur that is impossible to re-create.

The wall surrounding the estate is some 33km long, the same length as the *périphérique* (ring road) that surrounds Paris; the forest that it encloses is alive with wild boar and deer. The grounds are freely open to the public, only half of whom bother to go into the château itself. Enjoy Chambord at dawn or dusk, when mist emphasises the tiara-like roof enrichments.
Near Bracieux, 52km southwest of Orléans

off the D951, south of the Loire. Tel: 54 20 31 21. Open: daily. Son et lumière show from mid-April to mid-October (tel: 54 20 34 86 for details). Admission charge.

WRITERS OF THE LOIRE

For centuries, the Loire Valley has attracted writers. English diarist John Evelyn went to Tours to perfect his French, Beaumarchais (who wrote *The Barber of Seville*) lived in Vouvray, while Rousseau stayed in Chenonceau and Voltaire in Sully.

François Villon (1431–89)
Born François de Montcorbier, Villon is best-remembered for his irreverent and humorous writing, though his *Epitaphe Villon* is a serious plea for the compassionate treatment of criminals; he himself was convicted of manslaughter in 1455 and was imprisoned in Meung-sur-Loire (see page 101).

François Rabelais (1494–1553)
First a monk, then a doctor, Rabelais will always be remembered for his brilliant satirical books, *Gargantua* (1534) and *Pantagruel* (1532) in which he entertained the middle classes but shocked theologians by treating serious ideas within an often irreverent context.

Sobering thought: Rabelais surveys Chinon

Pierre de Ronsard (1524–85)
Born in La Possonnière near Vendôme on the Loir, Ronsard was plagued by deafness, so he left diplomatic life and settled at St-Cosme, near Tours where he penned his sonnets and odes, which, in their time, were not well received. Now his works, especially his love poems, are appreciated for their freshness and lyricism.

Honoré de Balzac (1799–1850)
Balzac was the chief exponent of the realistic novel. Many were scathing insights into the hypocracy of the French society of his time. He grew up in Tours and Vendôme, and frequently returned to Saché, near Chinon, to write and recharge his batteries after the excesses of Parisian life.

Max Jacob (1876–1944)
Poet, artist and friend of Picasso, Jacob left the Bohemian life of Montmartre for the solitude of St-Benoît-sur-Loire. A Jewish convert to Catholicism, he was deported by the Nazis and died in a concentration camp before his friends could rescue him.

Maurice Genevoix
(1890–1980)
Elected to the Academie Française in 1946, this prolific writer's best-known novel is *Raboliot*, the tale of a Sologne poacher. He lived at St-Denis-de-l'Hôtel.

Above: Balzac, social commentator
Above right: Scene from Verne's *Twenty Thousand Leagues Under the Sea* (1865)

Jules Verne (1828–1905)
Growing up in Nantes, Jules Verne's appetite for adventure, inspired by the busy quays, later gave rise to the new genre of science fiction, in such gripping works as *Twenty Thousand Leagues Under the Sea* (1865) and *Around the World in Eighty Days* (1873).

Henri Alain-Fournier (1886–1914)
See page 124.

Yesterday's glory: the garden and museum at Châteauneuf-sur-Loire

CHAMEROLLES, CHÂTEAU DE
Recently restored, the château at Chamerolles is now dedicated to sweet smells, with explanations of the manufacture and distillation of perfume and a collection of historic scent bottles. Even the gardens are planted with aromatic herbs, spices and flowers.
At Chilleurs-aux-Bois, 30km northeast of Orléans off the N152. Tel: 38 39 84 66. Open: daily. Closed: Tuesday. Admission charge.

CHÂTEAUDUN
The citizens of Châteaudun were collectively awarded the Legion d'Honneur (France's highest award) after 900 defenders held out against a Prussian force of 12,000 in 1870. For centuries, this rocky outcrop above the Loir has been a strategic stronghold, its daunting 45m-high, 12th-century keep one of the first to be built with rounded walls. Next to it, the Ste-Chapelle boasts 12 life-sized, painted statues, carved in the mid-15th century: St Agnés is

portrayed with a lamb and St Apollonia, patron saint of surgeons, holds a tooth and forceps. In the château, the Dunois Wing is named after the Comte who was one of Joan of Arc's most faithful comrades-in-arms. Gothic, gaunt and bare (without furniture, but hung with tapestries), this contrasts with the richly decorated Renaissance Longueville wing.
51km northwest of Orléans on the D955. Château – tel: 37 45 22 70. Open: daily. Admission charge.

CHÂTEAUNEUF-SUR-LOIRE
This affluent-looking dormitory town, just east of Orléans, has suffered twice: the French Revolution saw the destruction of its mini-version of Versailles, and World War II brought aerial bombing. Two attractions survived: in the château gardens, designed by Le Nôtre, the rhododendrons thrive, while in the old guardroom of the château, the Loire Nautical Museum records the river's shipbuilders and sailors, and their craft, the flat-bottomed *gabarres*, *chalands* and *sapines*.
25km east of Orléans on the Loire. Musée de la Marine de Loire – tel: 38 58 41 18. Open: July and August, Wednesday to Monday 10am–noon and 2–6pm; Wednesday to Monday in June, 2–6pm only. Admission charge.

CHEVERNY, CHÂTEAU DE
The ancestors of Charles-Antoine, Marquis de Vibraye, who now lives at Cheverny, built the first castle some seven centuries ago. Nothing now remains of the earlier fortress: what visitors tour is a majestic mansion of white stone, familiar to fans of the *Tintin* cartoons as Moulinsart the (imaginary) home of Captain Haddock. Cheverny is also known for its hunting tradition. The

kennels house a pack of 100 brown-and-white hounds, a cross between English foxhounds and Poitevins.

From a distance, the façade looks plain; closer inspection reveals busts of 12 Roman emperors in niches between the first-floor windows, and a 13th, Julius Caesar, in the gable above the central doorway. The guided tour begins in the dining-room, dominated by a table seating 30; castors of bone allow each chair to glide into place. Above, the silver-plated bronze chandelier looks modern but is 200 years old and weighs 100kg. The walls are covered in leather with 34 paintings, detailing the tale of Don Quixote.

Climbing upstairs, you will pass the antlers of a massive prehistoric moose, hung at its estimated height, 3m above the floor. In the 17th-century Armoury, children are intrigued by the 40kg battle armour, the locks on the pirate's chest and the miniature breastplate and helmet of the five-year-old Comte de Chambord. All grand châteaux had to have a Chambre du Roi, in case the king came to stay. Although King Henri IV did sleep in this bed, it was not in this room but in the earlier château on this site.

Top: Château de Cheverny
Right: Time and motion: Cheverny clock tells date, day, month and … time

Downstairs, a small bronze equestrian statue of George Washington faces a portrait of Louis XVI: they jointly founded the Order of Cincinnati to honour French and American officers who fought the English in the American War of Independence. In World War II, the Orangery in the garden was used to shelter French art treasures, including the *Mona Lisa*.

65km southwest of Orléans, 13km south of Blois. Tel: 54 79 96 29. Open: daily. Admission charge.

TARTE TATIN

Lamotte-Beuvron, a pleasant little town in the Solongne, 35km south of Orléans, is where the Tatin sisters 'invented' their famous caramelised apple tart in the 1850s. Like so many famous dishes, it was created by mistake. On discovering that the pastry to line the dish had been forgotten, Caroline spread it on *top* of the apples, butter and sugar. After baking, she inverted the pie and discovered … *Tarte Tatin*. Now Gilles Caillé, at the Hôtel Tatin, opposite the station, produces a dozen a day, using locally grown *reinette*, *clochard* or *golden* apples. Tradition insists that there should be no cream, no jam and no *flambé*-ing.

CLÉRY-ST-ANDRÉ

Medieval pilgrims thronged here after a statue of the Virgin Mary was found in a bush in 1280. The original church was razed by the English in 1438 but Louis XI (1423–83) revived the shrine, pledging his weight in silver to the Virgin. His skull, and that of his wife, are locked away in a glass case; under a nearby stone is the heart of their son, Charles VIII, who finished the rebuilding. *15km southwest of Orléans on the D951. For access to the mausoleum, contact the presbytery at 1 rue du Cloître, next to the basilica. Tel: 38 45 70 05.*

FERTÉ-ST-AUBIN, CHÂTEAU DE LA

This offers more than many other Loire Valley châteaux. The big draw is the cookery demonstration in the vaulted, stone-floored, 17th-century kitchen. A log fire blazes, game and vegetables are heaped on the massive work table and Marthe, the cook, in bonnet and apron, conjures up *terrines* and *tartes tatins* (see box) using the gleaming copper pots. Outside, the petting zoo and the real horses in the historic stables occupy the children while the adults tour the 18 rooms of the 16th-century château. *18km south of Orléans on the N20. Tel: 38 76 52 72. Open: mid-March to mid-November, daily 10am–7pm. Cooking demonstrations daily, April to September, but phone to check. Admission charge.*

GERMIGNY-DES-PRÉS

Germigny-des-Prés has one of the oldest

Small is beautiful: locals claim Germigny-des-Prés's church is the oldest in France

surviving churches in France, built in AD806 and beautifully decorated with 130,000 gold, silver and blue cubes of glittering glass to form a Byzantine picture of the Ark of the Covenant, guarded by the Hand of God and four angels. In the squat lantern tower above the altar thin panes of translucent alabaster, rather than glass, fill the windows.
28km southeast of Orléans on the Loire. Tel: 38 58 27 30. Open daily. Donation appreciated.

MENNETOU-SUR-CHER

Mennetou is a delightful town of steep and twisting streets set within 800-year-old walls, still standing over 12m high. The Porte d'en Bas is often called the Porte Jeanne d'Arc, for she stopped here on 3 March, 1429, on her way to Chinon to see the Dauphin (see page 92). The Grande-Rue is actually a narrow lane, lined with ancient houses, including the tourist office, which occupies a 16th-century layer-cake of sandy stone and half-timbering, topped with red tiles, next to another massive gate.
85km south of Orléans on the N76.

MEUNG-SUR-LOIRE

'Remember poor Villon,' the poet and rascal, François Villon (see page 96) implored his friends from the castle dungeon. He was reprieved in 1461, by Louis XI, but hundreds of less-fortunate inmates died here. Take a look at the *salle de question* (a euphemism for torture chamber) and the *oubliettes*, where 'forgotten' prisoners starved to death. Most of the rest of the château was remodelled in the 18th century.

The village, where the Mauve river splits into rivulets and channels before joining the Loire, is also known for the 13th-century poet, Jean de Meung, who added 18,000 new lines to the *Roman de la Rose* (written by Guillame de Lorris around 1240). His satirical style criticised the conventions of courtly love and morals of self-indulgent priests. No wonder it was hugely popular.
22km southwest of Orléans on the N152. Tel: 38 44 25 61. Open: daily, April to October. Admission charge.

Left: Meung's menacing dungeon
Below: the Porte d'Amont, Meung-sur-Loire

Country life: an elegant sitting-room in the remote Château du Moulin

MOULIN, CHÂTEAU DU

Off the beaten tourist track, this château has a wide moat, drawbridge and towers with loopholes, crenellations and machicolations. It is, however, more country mansion than fortress. At the battle of Fornovo di Taro, in 1495, Philippe du Moulin saved the life of Charles VIII; the grateful monarch awarded his captain the privilege of fortifying his home. The two surviving buildings sit on a large, square terrace. Inside, 14th-century tapestries hang in the main bedroom with its curtained four-poster bed, and the main salon has a painted ceiling, while handsome pewter flagons and platters sit on a heavily carved sideboard. There is even an original spit, which would once have been powered by a dog.

65km southwest of Orléans off the D765, near Lassay-sur-Croisne. Tel: 54 83 83 51. Open: daily. Closed: mid-November to end-February. Admission charge.

QUINCY AND REUILLY

These two neighbouring, and somewhat undistinguished, villages produce good but little-known wines. The best from Quincy are the dry white Sauvignons, made in the Sancerre style. Reuilly produces reds and *rosés* and has a wine festival in the first weekend of April.

Quincy is on the west bank of the Cher, 104km south of Orléans.
Reuilly is on the D198, 110km south of Orléans.

ROMORANTIN-LANTHENAY

Built on and around an island in the Sauldre river, the 'capital of the Sologne' offers pleasant walks by old watermills and crooked streets lined by 15th- and 16th-century timber-framed houses. Head for the rue du Milieu where, at the Maison du Carroir D'Orré, a carved St George raises his sword to slay the dragon. Near by, the Hôtel St-Pol is a handsome mixture of glazed bricks and stone. Here, on 6 January, 1521, François I was up to some high jinks when he was hit on the head by a burning log. The 26-year-old king grew a beard to hide the scar, and set a new fashion. Opposite, La Chancellerie boasts a finely carved bagpiper. The

Motor Racing Museum shows locally built blue Matra racing cars, including Jackie Stewart's MS 80.

65km south of Orléans on the D922. Musée Municipal de la Course Automobile, rue Faubourg d'Orléans. Tel: 54 76 07 06. Open: daily, mid-March to mid-November. Closed: Sunday morning and Tuesday. Free.

ST-BENOÎT-SUR-LOIRE

Dominating the village is the massive abbey church of St-Benoît, the final resting place of St Benedict (480–547), the father of western monasticism. The

simplicity, solid and impressive. The recumbent statue of Philippe I of France (1052–1108) lies by the altar, and steps down to the darkened crypt on the left lead to St Benedict's relics, housed in a brass-bound metal chest. The monks offer guided tours, and it is well worth staying for one of the six daily services in Gregorian chant.

40km southeast of Orléans off the D952. Tel: 38 35 72 43.

Below: Romorantin-Lanthenay
Below right: the abbey of St-Benoît

Italian saint died at Montecassino, near Naples, but when that monastery was sacked, his remains were transferred to this site in AD672. The present church was built between 1067 and 1218. Twelve massive pillars support the bell-tower-cum-porch, each heavily carved with scenes from the *Book of Revelations*. The design reflects John's vision in Revelations 21, with three doors or arches to the east, west, north and south.

The interior of the church, 73m long and 20m high, is a model of Romanesque

The Château at Sully

Selles' patron saint, Eusice, who arrived in the 6th century. In the main square, the simple Cher Valley Museum of local life focuses on basket-weaving, flint-cutting and the fine local goat's cheese. The flat round discs, salted and dusted in crushed charcoal, are well-partnered by Côtes du Cher wines, red or white.
100km southwest of Orléans off the N76. Château – tel: 54 97 63 98. Open: daily. Actors perform July to mid-September. Admission charge.
Musée du Val de Cher – tel: 54 97 40 19. Open: daily, Whitsun to mid-September. Closed: Monday. Admission charge.

SOUVIGNY-EN-SOLOGNE

This Sologne hamlet is famous for its half-timbered and red-brick houses and its church, which has a vast red-tiled roof and unusual 16th-century *caquetoir* (covered porch, so-called because parishioners gathered here to gossip.
37km southeast of Orléans, east of Lamotte-Beuvron.

SELLES-SUR-CHER

A small town with big ideas, Selles promotes itself as a holiday base. Less than an hour's drive from a dozen famous châteaux it also invites anglers to try the four waterways that flow round and through the town. The dilapidated-looking moated château is under repair, but it comes to life during the summer when 10 actors playing the Duc de Sully and Catherine de'Medici, plus assorted cooks, musicians and messengers, re-create 17th-century château life. Part farm, part medieval fortress, part Renaissance mansion, it has memorabilia of the Polish royal family and the Count of Chambord, the 19th-century pretender to the French throne.

The former abbey church, with its energetic sculptures, is the burial place of

Village gossip: the covered porch at Souvigny-en-Sologne

SULLY-SUR-LOIRE

Sully is a microcosm of French history, boasting a roll-call of famous residents. One was Maurice de Sully, a poor local priest who went to Paris, became bishop and commissioned the building of Nôtre-Dame cathedral. Three centuries later, Joan of Arc arrived to take the Dauphin, Charles VII, to Reims to be crowned.

The town's heyday came after Maximilien de Béthune (1560–1641), Henri IV's chief minister, bought the estate and became the Duc de Sully in the early 17th century. Like a modern tycoon, he was up before sunrise, with a rota of secretaries recording his orders. Learned in law and accountancy, he had a secret printing press installed in one tower to print his memoirs, entitled *Wise and Royal Economies of State*.

His château is undergoing massive restoration, which actually adds to the interest of a visit. The first floor was converted into a theatre when an 18th-century descendant of the duke welcomed the banished 22-year-old playwright, François-Marie Arouet, to his home. Arouet later adopted the pen-name Voltaire, and he wrote several plays here in the early 1700s. At night the moated castle is dramatically floodlit.

41km southeast of Orléans on the D948.
Château – tel: 38 36 86 86. Open: daily, March to October. Admission charge.

Left: tableau at Selles-sur-Cher

TALCY, CHÂTEAU DE

Two women inspired two different poets in this delightful fortified Gothic-style manor. The first was Cassandra, the 15-year-old daughter of Tuscan banker, Bernardo Salviati, who bought the château in 1517. Ronsard (1524–85) dedicated over 180 of his frustrated love poems to this 'nymph'. Salviati's grand-daughter, Diana, had the same effect on Agrippa d'Aubigné (1552–1630) who dedicated his poem *Le Printemps* (*Springtime*) to her. The Renaissance rooms are full of fine furniture, and there is an ingenious mechanical wine-press, still in working order, in the cellar, as well as a dovecote with two rotating ladders to reach up to the 1,500 nesting boxes.

40km southwest of Orléans off the A10, D70. Château – tel: 54 81 03 01. Open: daily. Closed: Tuesday in winter. Admission charge.

The Duke of Sully, one of France's finest administrators

TROUSSAY, CHÂTEAU DE

A century ago, the historian, Louis de la Saussaye, set out to save treasures from dilapidated mansions. His collection, including Renaissance stained glass and a stone carving of a porcupine from Blois, now enlivens his manor house near Cheverny. A small museum of Sologne life, with agricultural implements, is housed in the outbuildings.

70km southwest of Orléans off the D765, 3.5km west of Cheverny. Tel: 54 44 29 07. Open: June to August, daily 10am–12.30pm and 2–7pm; May and September to mid-November, Sunday and public holidays only 10.30am–12.30pm and 2–6pm. Admission charge.

VALENÇAY, CHÂTEAU DU

Charles-Maurice de Talleyrand-Périgord, better known simply as Talleyrand, purchased Valençay in 1803, when he was Napoleon's Foreign Minister, and he used the château to entertain dignitaries from all over Europe. After the fall of Napoleon, negotiations under the Congress of Vienna (1814–15) were held here to redraw the map of Europe. Talleyrand's influence was greatly increased by the skill of his chef, Marie-Antoine Carême, who is represented here by a waxwork figure in the kitchen. A bedroom with Talleyrand's own furniture is a recent addition. The fine gardens have black swans, deer, peacocks and cranes. A museum in the park displays 70 classic cars, all in working order. The summer programme includes concerts, plays and *son et lumière*.

115km southwest of Orléans on the D956. Tel: 54 00 10 66. Open: daily, March to November. Admission charge.
Son et lumière shows based on the story of Beauty and the Beast *in July, August and September (tel: 54 00 14 33 for details).*

Automania: Valençay reflects the French love affair with the car

St George's Gate: home of Vendôme's Council Chamber for 400 years

VENDÔME

Now a mere 40 minutes from Paris by TGV, the so-called 'gateway to the Loire' honours the famous people who lived here with a bust of the 16th-century poet, Ronsard, in rue St-Jacques, and a statue on the place St-Martin of the Comte de Rochambeau, who helped the American colonists defeat the British at the Battle of Yorktown in 1781. The 19th-century author, Honoré de Balzac, spent miserable schooldays here, but still used the town as a setting for such novels as *Louis Lambert*.

Remnants of the medieval era include the castle on the hill and La Trinité Church, founded by the Count and Countess of Anjou after seeing a vision of three flaming spears (or shooting stars) in 1035. The 80m bell tower, with its 11-ton bell, dates from this early church, but the west front is an outstanding example of Flamboyant Gothic architecture, with stonework that really does look flame-like. The most arresting of the stained-glass windows is the 12th-century *Virgin and Child* at the eastern end; most fun are the carved angels and devils on the misericords, in the choir.

76km southwest of Orléans on the N10. Château – tel: 54 77 05 07. Open: daily. Admission charge.

VILLESAVIN, CHÂTEAU DE

Villesavin was built between 1526 and 1537 by Jean le Breton, the financial advisor to François I, and superintendent of the building works at nearby Chambord. Now, a bumpy driveway leads to his small château, which encloses a courtyard with a white Carrara-marble basin, carved by the same Italians who built the rest of the charming Renaissance building. The original dovecote is in excellent condition, complete with ladder and 1,500 nesting boxes.

60km southwest of Orléans, near Bracieux. Tel: 54 46 42 88. Open: daily March to Christmas; afternoons only October to late December. Admission charge.

Old Orléans

This short stroll provides insights into the history of the former capital of France. *Allow 45 minutes.*

Start facing the main entrance of Ste-Croix cathedral. Turn right, passing a statue representing the Loire, and enter the old quarter along rue Parisie. Take the second turning on the right.

1 RUE DE BOURGOGNE

Now pedestrianised, this was once the main Roman street, and Joan of Arc would have ridden down it in 1429 (see page 92). The circular church on the right, covered with carved angels' faces, dates from 1837. Number 261 is a fine medieval mix of brick, timber and stone, while No 264 (opposite) is now a British-style pub. Spot the modern *trompe l'oeil* above the intersection with rue de la Cholerie.
Turn right on to rue Ste-Catherine.

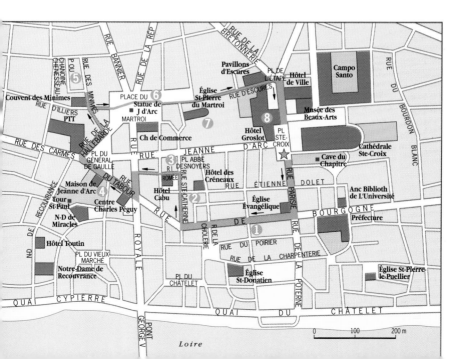

2 HÔTEL DES CRENEAUX

Now used by music students at the
Conservatoire, this 15th-century
mansion was, until 1790, the town hall.
The belfry next door dates from 1445.
Turn left on rue Isabelle Romée

3 PLACE ABBÉ DESNOYERS

Behind the belfry on this new square is
the stone façade of the Renaissance
Maison de la Pomme, boasting carved
faces and the apple after which it is
named. Across the square, the house
built by Philippe Cabu in 1548 was
nicknamed the Maison de Diane de
Poitiers after the mistress of Henry II
stayed here. Now it houses the History
Museum (see page 90).
*Turn left on rue Royale, pausing to admire
the highly decorated Hôtel Euverte Hatte,
now the Charles Péguy Cultural Centre.
Turn right on rue du Tabour.*

4 MAISON DE JEANNE D'ARC

On the corner of the place du Général de
Gaulle, the Maison de Jeanne d'Arc
looks medieval, but is a careful copy of
Jacques Boucher's home, where Joan
stayed in 1429 (see page 91). Next door,
the Maison de la Porte Renard is
genuinely 15th-century, while an arch on
the right leads to the peaceful garden
surrounding the Pavillon Colas des
Francs, a 16th-century counting-house.
*Cross place du Général de Gaulle. Turn left
on rue des Minimes.*

5 COUVENT DES MINIMES

Opposite the Orléans rugby club
headquarters, look down the Passage du
Chanoine Chenesseau for glimpses of the
17th-century arches of the convent, now
the Archives Museum.
*Retrace your steps, then turn left on rue
d'Illiers into the city's main square.*

Intricate iron lace-work, Orléans

6 PLACE DU MARTROI

Follow the story of Joan of Arc as carved
on the base of her romantic, 19th-
century statue. To the right, the
handsome Chancellerie (1759) is where
the Duke of Orléans kept his paperwork
200 years ago.
Leave the square on the rue d'Escures.

7 ÉGLISE ST-PIERRE DU MARTROI

Guarded by lime trees, this is the city's
only brick church. Grand houses line
the street. On the left, the Pavillons
d'Escures, a fine 17th-century town-
house development, was inspired by the
mayor, Pierre Fougeu d'Escures. On the
right, the Groslot garden has a porch
surviving from the St-Jacques pilgrims's
chapel that once stood by the Loire.
*At the end of rue d' Escures, turn right on
to the place de l'Étape.*

8 HÔTEL GROSLOT

Built for the city bailiff in 1555, this was
given a Gothic Revival facelift 300 years
later. A greenish-bronze statue of Joan of
Arc stands in front of the hôtel, which
served as the town hall from 1790 to
1982. The present town hall stands
opposite.

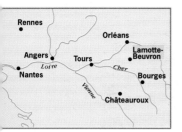

The Sologne

The once marshy, but now drained, Sologne has
long been a mysterious part of France. Today, the
region is famous for hunting, the red-brick villages
are quiet and unspoiled and, because it is flat,
cycling is straightforward. *Allow two days or, taking the short-cut indicated, one long day.*

Start in Lamotte-Beuvron, by the railway station.

1 HÔTEL TATIN

Tarte Tatin, the famous apple tart, originated here (see page
100). A wedge of this should fortify any cyclist.
*Head north, past the town hall. Take the D101 for Vouzon, through
the Lamotte-Beuvron forest.*

2 VOUZON

The houses here are of warm-coloured brick with red-tiled roofs.
*Turn right before the church, still on the D101. In summer, the
roadside is ablaze with purple heather.*

3 SOUVIGNY-EN-SOLOGNE

This village of 400 inhabitants has a photogenic church, built
between the 12th and 17th centuries. A sharp spire juts from the
red-tiled roof; the well-preserved *caquetoir* (see page 104) dates
from the 16th century. Among the surrounding half-timbered
houses are two good restaurants: the Auberge de la Croix
Blanche (tel: 54 88 40 08) and the gourmet Perdrix Rouge (tel:
54 88 41 05) – see pages 168-9.
Take the D126 for Chaon.

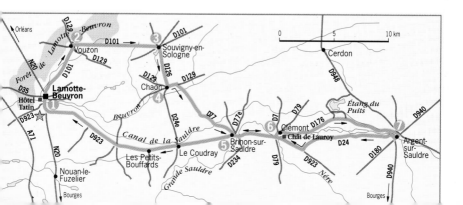

4 CHAON

The road leads through pleasant countryside, past a château with half-timbered stables, ponds and picnickers. Chaon is another pretty red-brick village. *Continue on the D126, then turn on to the D77 for Brinon.*

5 BRINON-SUR-SAULDRE

Children are often to be seen swimming in the Sauldre river, which flows through the village and into the Cher. The church, set on a rise, has a distinctive spire, a deep-sweeping roof and another *caquetoir*. *From here, it is possible to take a short cut back to Lamotte-Beuvron via the D923. Otherwise, continue, still on the D923, to Clémont.*

6 CLÉMONT

A giant grain elevator signals the entrance to Clémont, which is just off the main road, set round a triangular village green. The Auberge de la Corne du Cerf, with its stag's heads and hunting-lodge look is a cool retreat in summer. The 14th-century church is unusual in this area in being built of stone, rather than brick. *To the right of the Auberge, take the D176 towards Cerdon, but turn sharp right along the river for Argent-sur-Sauldre, beneath shady plane trees.*

Top: Antiques workshops in Argent-sur-Sauldre
Above: The River Sauldre near Brinon

7 ARGENT-SUR-SAULDRE

On the left, the 100-year-old Étang du Puits is both bird sanctuary and leisure park, with windsurfers on the lake. Enter Argent by crossing both the canal and the river to find two rival *auberges*, both covered with flowers. In the château, the old-fashioned but interesting Musée des Métiers et Traditions (Trades and Traditions) commemorates the everyday life of the *ventres jaunes* (yellow bellies), as the Sologne people are nicknamed. Discover the uses of strange-looking implements such as the *tourniquet de bébé* – not a medical tool but a baby walker. *Return to Clémont on the D24, south of the river, then via Brinon back to Lamotte-Beuvron on the D923.*

The Cher

This route explores a short quiet stretch of the
south bank of the Cher. The river is 367km long,
but this drive is only some 87km, from Vierzon to
Montrichard. *Allow at least half a day.*

1 VIERZON

This dull, industrial town has hidden corners of
interest. Known today for its porcelain, it has long been a
watery intersection where the Yèvre meets the Cher. In the old
town, narrow streets lined with medieval houses lead to the
12th-century church of Nôtre-Dame.
Go south on the D918, then the D918e, following signs for St-
Hilaire-de-Court and then St-Georges-sur-la-Prée. Continue on
the D50 and D51 to St-Julien. On the way, note the dramatic
Anjou-style spire of the St-Loup church (inside are 13th-century
murals).

2 ST-JULIEN-SUR-CHER

The peace and quiet of St-Julien contrasts with its neighbour
Villefranche, across the bridge, where lorries constantly rumble
through on the main road.
Continue on the D51, then take the D35 to Chabris.

3 CHABRIS

Chabris is a jolly little village, with a riverside campsite under
the trees where children dive into the Cher. Rent a bicycle and
pedal by the river, have a glass of Sauvignon wine and local
goat's cheese or go dancing at the *guinguette*, the dance hall-
cum-café. St-Phalien, a 5th-century hermit, is buried in the
church which boasts unusual criminal carvings.
Continue on the D35, then take the D51 to Selles.

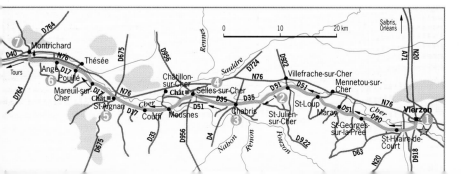

On guard for 1,000 years: Foulques III Nerra's keep at Montrichard

4 SELLES-SUR-CHER

Famous for its goat's cheeses the town has several half-timbered houses as well as the remains of the 6th-century hermit, St-Eusice, buried in the crypt of the 12th-century church (see page 104). The former Abbaye Royale houses a Museum of the Cher with displays on the local boatmen and the making of goat's cheese. The town's 17th-century château comes to life from July to September. Beware the costumed actors who lock some visitors in the prison!
Take the D17 to St-Aignan, passing through Meusnes which, for 300 years, was the centre of the gunflints industry.

5 ST-AIGNAN-SUR-CHER

St-Aignan's church is a mix of Norman and Gothic architecture with intricately carved pillars and, in the vast crypt, 12th-century frescos depicting miracle cures worked by medieval saints. The town's 16th-century château is closed to the public, but its courtyard offers a vista over the town's medieval rooftops.

Getting there involves a climb of 114 steps up a curving, stone staircase.
Continue on the D17 to Pouillé.

6 POUILLÉ

This wine-producing town is surrounded by Touraine vineyards, devoted to growing Sauvignon Blanc and Gamay grapes. Pouillé's Gamay Festival is held on the last Sunday in July.
Continue on the D17 and cross the bridge to Montrichard.

7 MONTRICHARD

Above the town (see page 72) stands the restored keep of Foulques III Nerra where Richard the Lionheart was besieged by Philippe-August in 1188. The graffiti on the walls were left by the Knights Templar in 1308. The Church of Ste-Croix hosted the ill-fated marriage of Jeanne, the deformed daughter of Louis XI, and the Duke of Orleans, later Louis XII.
Return to Tours on the D40, on the northern bank of the Cher, or the faster N76, on the southern bank.

The Eastern Loire

*B*ourges, famous for its majestic cathedral, one of the greatest Gothic creations in France, is the largest city in the Eastern Loire. Bourges and the surrounding region of Berry are surprisingly overlooked when it comes to visitors. 'Many French aren't sure where we are,' admits one local, 'they think we're further south.' But this area is the centre of France and is not short of history.

The city is also associated with Jacques Coeur (1400–56), skilful financial adviser to Charles VII. His is one of the finest medieval mansions in France but there are plenty of others, albeit less grand, on the cobbled streets of the old quarter.

Built by Eiffel: the Briare canal bridge

The countryside around Bourges has few 'attractions' in the tourist sense. The flat Sologne is popular with hunters, and it has several churches with *caquetoirs* (porches 'for gossiping'), surrounded by red-brick cottages. Sancerre and Pouilly are renowned for their flinty, dry white wines around the world.

The region also has its surprises. One is the iron canal aqueduct that spans the Loire at Briare; another is the 16th-century bridge, with 10 arches, at nearby La Charité. Turn up in Aubigny-sur-Nère in mid-July and you will hear the skirl of the pipes and see the lilt of the kilt as Scottish visitors confirm the Auld Alliance; the Verrerie, a nearby château, was built by one John Stuart, who battled with the French against the English.

Another château, at La Bussière, is devoted to all aspects of angling, while the early owners of the château at La Chapelle d'Angillon discovered a tax loophole that today's accountants would relish. The work of the craftsmen-potters

THE DUC DE BERRY

The beautifully illuminated calendar, known as *Les Très Riches Heures du Duc De Berry*, depicts several places in the Loire Valley that are recognisable even today. First comes January, with the Duc de Berry himself seated at a well-laden dining-table, surrounded by a retinue dressed in the latest medieval fashion. September depicts the *vendange* (grape harvest) below the château at Saumur. Created by the Limbourg brothers and paid for by their patron, Jean, Duc de Berry (1340–1416), the original is now preserved at the Musée Condé in Chantilly, north of Paris.

THE EASTERN LOIRE

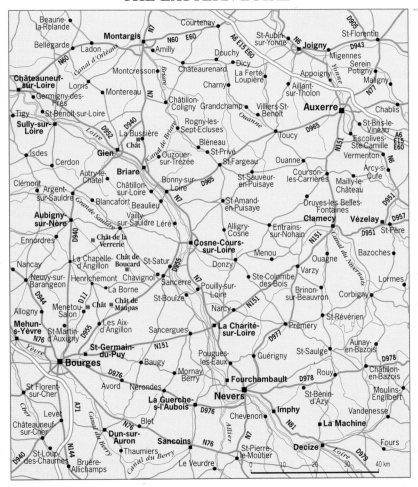

at La Borne contrasts with the stylised designs on the faïence of Gien. Deep in the country, Nançay offers art galleries and a gentleman's tailor catering to chic Parisians on weekend getaways. At the eastern extreme of the area is Nevers, a town worth a visit in its own right, but often overrun with pilgrims visiting the convent where St Bernadette (of Lourdes fame) lies embalmed.

Bourges

*O*nly in 1992, when Bourges cathedral was named a World Heritage site by UNESCO, did this well-preserved medieval city finally get its deserved share of the limelight. Until then, even the French thought of Bourges as being '*dans la France profonde*', deep in provincial France. Part of this lack of recognition is due to the city fathers of 150 years ago who rejected the offer of a railway line. Even today, there are only two direct trains a day to Paris; otherwise, the locals have to change in Vierzon, 35km to the north.

Bourges is much more than its cathedral, however: the city was founded by the Romans and was later the capital of Aquitaine. In the 14th and 15th centuries, Bourges benefited from royal patronage. Nothing remains of the magnificent palace built by Jean, Duc de Berry (1340–1416), the brother of Charles V. The Duke was a lover of luxury and culture, and his tubby effigy marks his tomb in the cathedral crypt. His great-nephew, the weak, uncrowned Charles VII, was forced to flee here from Paris. He was mockingly nicknamed the 'Little King of Bourges', whereas Henry VI of England was called the 'King of Paris' because of his legitimate claim to the French throne and his effective control over most of France.

Bourges, however, remained a centre of resistance to the English in the final years of the Hundred Years' War, even before the arrival of Joan of Arc. The king's financier, the merchant banker, Jacques Coeur, planned to live here and he built a mansion as fine, if not finer, than any royal palace (though he never actually spent a night under its roof). The city's commercial power matched that of Lyon and Rouen and its university was founded in 1463. Jean Calvin, the Protestant reformer, studied here in the 16th century, when new theological ideas from Germany were taking hold in France. As elsewhere, the Wars of Religion took their toll, with a fire in 1487 that destroyed much of the city.

Today, Bourges is still a capital, but only of the *département* of Cher. With a population of 92,000, it is a compact city whose April festival, Printemps de Bourges (Bourges Spring), focuses on French song. The economy depends on modern industries such as aeronautics, electronics, tyres and armaments; the last is nothing new, since Jacques Coeur traded arms to the Middle East as early as the 15th century.

BURGHERS OF BOURGES
The people of Angers are called Angevins; those in Tours are Tourangeaux; in Orléans, they are Orléanais. In Bourges you might expect them to be Bourgeois but, in fact, they are Berruyers.

Sixty-five metres up the cathedral's North Tower

Cathédrale de St-Étienne

On statistics alone, the cathedral is enormously impressive: 124m long, 41m wide and 37.5m high with 1,000sq m of stained glass. St-Étienne stands shoulder-to-shoulder with Notre-Dame de Paris, Chartres and Reims as a jewel of Gothic architecture, thanks to the consistency of style, intricate stone carving and the richly coloured 13th- and 15th-century windows.

The harmony was achieved by the speed of construction: most of the building went up in a mere 60 years, beginning in 1195, but was finally finished in 1324. Today, only the disparate height of the towers spoils the symmetry. Stand in the boulevard de Strasbourg in the morning to appreciate the *chevet* (the eastern end of the church) with its five radiating chapels and its two tiers of flying buttresses. Climb the 396

because it was funded by 'indulgences' paid by affluent townsfolk for the privilege of eating butter during Lent. The 58m Tour Sourde (Deaf Tower), on the right, got its name from being soundless – it never did have its bells installed. Both had spires which have collapsed; the Butter Tower has been rebuilt, while the Deaf Tower is supported by a buttress built in the 14th century.

The west façade is dense with sculptures. From left to right are the portals dedicated to St-Guillaume (a 13th-century archbishop of Bourges), the Virgin Mary, the Last Judgement, St-Étienne and St-Ursin, the first bishop of Bourges. The message of the Last Judgement is as clear now as it was to illiterate folk 800 years ago. Figures emerge from their tombs and clamber up to see what is happening on the next level. The Archangel Michael, smiling broadly,

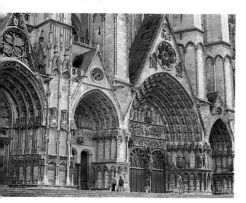

well-worn steps that lead to the top of the 65m-high North (or Butter) Tower. From here, the nave really does look like an upturned ship.

Before going into the main entrance, stop and look at the west front. The Butter Tower, to the left, is so named

Far left: St-Étienne's west front; left: window in crypt; above: cathedral *chevet*

weighs the souls. To the left, off go the good souls to the bosom of Abraham; to the right, a delighted demon takes his victim to join the other unfortunates on their way to meet the devil. Monks are judged and found wanting; a toad pulls out tongues.

Inside, there are five naves to match the five portals. The late 14th-century west window features in the *Très Riches Heures* (see page 114). A copper strip set diagonally across the floor shows where the Paris meridian slices through the building, and a two-faced astrological clock dates from 1424. In the choir, the triumphant sense of light and space is due to the delicate pillars being slightly staggered. Between 10 and 11am on a sunny morning, the sun pours through the 12th-century stained-glass windows, which feel almost close enough to touch.

These, too, have tales to tell. Some were sponsored by local guilds, such as the butchers or furriers, and illustrate appropriate events in the Bible. The story of the Prodigal Son, sixth from the left, has figures dancing the *pavane*, cheek to cheek. High above the altar, two faded cardinal's hats hang from the roof. Local lore has it that the cardinals will languish in purgatory until the hats eventually rot and fall to the ground, when they will finally enter paradise. In the crypt, stonemasons work on the never-ending task of maintaining the building. Among the archbishops buried here is the recumbent marble effigy of Jean, Duc de Berry, guarded by a bear. *Open: daily. Guided tours (lasting 2 hours) from mid-July to the end of August.*

Hôtel Cujas (Musée du Berry)

This fine mansion was built in 1515 for a Florentine cloth merchant. Today it houses the Musée du Berry, best-known for its local Roman finds and Egyptian mummies. Here, too, are the *Pleurants*, mourning statues, which once surrounded the tomb of Jean, Duc de Berry, carved in the 14th century but remarkably modern in the simplicity.

4-6 rue des Arènes. Tel: 48 57 81 15. Open: daily. Closed: Tuesday, Sunday morning. Admission charge.

Hôtel Lallemant

This Renaissance mansion is built on the remains of the Roman city wall. The broad entrance steps enabled horsemen to ride directly into the main courtyard, which is decorated with pottery plaques of classical heroes. In the family chapel, the ceiling is carved with alchemical symbols. Recently restored, this building is now a museum devoted to the decorative arts, ranging from tapestries and faïence to fine examples of carved, inlaid and lacquered furniture.

6 rue Bourbonnoux. Tel: 48 57 81 17. Open: daily. Closed: Tuesday, Sunday morning. Admission charge.

Hôtel des Echevins

Dramatically lit at night, this plain 15th-century L-shaped building, with its elaborate eight-sided stair turret, was built as a meeting place for the city aldermen. Now it is a showcase for the work of the local contemporary artist, Maurice Estève.

13 rue Edouard de Branly. Tel: 48 24 75 38. Open: daily; closed Tuesday, Sunday morning. Admission charge.

Palais Jacques-Coeur

Despite being unfurnished, this is one of the most interesting mansions in the whole of the Loire Valley. Jacques Coeur

spent an estimated 100,000 golden *écus* building his grand home. Arraigned in 1451, he never had a chance

Details of the Palais Jacques-Coeur

JACQUES COEUR (1395-1456)

'*A vaillans coeurs, riens impossible*' (To brave hearts, nothing is impossible); so ran the punning motto of one of the most powerful men in France. As counsellor to the king, he reformed the tax system and put France back on her financial feet after the drain of the Hundred Years' War. Coeur married well and he rose to become one of the richest men in Europe. His ships brought back silks and spices from the Middle East and he was soon in favour with Charles VII.

Coeur was less popular with royal courtiers when he took land and property from them as payment for outstanding debts. Since he had a powerful ally in the king's mistress, Agnès Sorel, this did not seem to matter. At her untimely death in 1450, however, he was arrested and fined one fifth of his fortune, even before the trial. The accusation? Supplying arms to the Muslims (infidels) and poisoning Sorel. Coeur was found guilty on all charges except the allegation of poisoning. The punishment was exile and confiscation of the rest of his fortune. Coeur escaped from prison in Poitiers and fled to Rome. He died, fighting in Rhodes against the Turks. Four years later, some justice was done when Louis XI threw out the court decision and returned Coeur's property to his family.

to enjoy it. From the strong room (complete with secret locks) to the kitchens, the architecture is ingenious. There is even a steam bath and toilet. The fine Galerie des Marchands, with its beamed, boat's keel roof, stands next door to the private chapel, where angels fly across the ceiling. In the dining-hall, the stone fireplace is as monumental as any in the region. Coeur's business ethic – *Dire, Faire, Taire* (Speak, Do and Be Silent) – is carved on the east façade of the palace. Visit early or late to avoid the crowds in summer.

rue Jacques-Coeur. Tel: 48 24 06 87. Open: daily. Admission charge.

Learn about life in the Sologne in the château at Argent-sur-Sauldre

ARGENT-SUR-SAULDRE

In this quiet Sologne village, the 15th-century château houses two museums. One is devoted to the Bulgarian Vassil Ivanoff, an influential 20th-century ceramicist, and the other looks at the ingenuity of the locals, nicknamed *les ventres-jaunes* (the yellow bellies) because of endemic jaundice. Their useful inventions include spiked collars to protect dogs from wolves, clogs elevated on spikes to keep feet dry in marshy conditions, and a charcoal-fuelled ancestor of the washing-machine.
57km north of Bourges, on the D940. Musée Vassil-Ivanoff – tel: 48 73 34 02. Open: May to mid-October, Monday to Friday 2–6.30pm, weekends 10am–noon and 2–6.30pm. Admission charge. Museé des Métiers et Traditions de France –
tel: 48 73 33 10. Open: July to late August, Monday to Saturday 2–6.30pm, Sunday 10am–noon and 2–6.30pm; May, June, September and October, daily 2–6.30pm. Admission charge.

AUBIGNY-SUR-NÈRE

On the weekend nearest Bastille Day, 14 July, the street parade through this *Cité des Stuarts* (Stuart City) includes twirling medieval banners and the *tricolore* of France, plus skirling bagpipes, swishing kilts and flags of St Andrew, celebrating the Auld Alliance victory against the English in 1419. All is explained in the town's small museum, dedicated to the alliance, which is housed in the town hall. Specially designed tartan, combining the colours of the town's shield with those of the Stuarts of Atholl, is for sale.

Centre d'Exposition de l'Auld Alliance – tel:
48 81 50 00. Open: daily, July to mid-
September; weekends only mid-September
to June. Admission charge.

Château de la Verrerie

Little of John Stuart's 15th-century
castle survives; the brick Renaissance
gallery, with its nine arches, and the
murals in the chapel were added by his
descendant, Robert Stuart. When the
family died out in 1670, Louis XIV gave
the château to the Duchess of
Portsmouth, mistress of Charles II of
England – himself a Stuart. More
impressive than in photographs, the
romantic setting by the reflecting lake
supposedly inspired scenes in Le Grand
Meaulnes, by local author Alain-
Fournier. The current owners, the
Comte and Comtesse de Vogüé, offer
up-market dinner-bed-and-breakfast
accommodation.
10km southeast of Aubigny on the D89.
Château – tel: 48 58 06 91. Open: daily,
March to November. Admission charge.

Aubigny is 50km north of Bourges on the
D940.

LA BORNE

Over 400 years ago, the local abundance
of clay and wood made La Borne a
centre for the making of everyday
stoneware vessels. This tradition died
out, only to be reborn in the 1940s when
a new generation of artists settled here.
Among the first were Monsieur and
Madame André Rosay, who continued
making pottery in the peasant style,
known as art populaire. Vassil Ivanoff (see
opposite) created clay figures and shapes.

Now some 50 craftsmen from eight
countries work in and around what is a
creative, if not a pretty, village. The
Centre de Céramique, in the former
girls' school, displays contemporary
works. Individual studios are open to
visitors.
37km northeast of Bourges on the D22.
Tel: 48 26 93 38. Open: daily. Free.

BOUCARD, CHÂTEAU DE

The River Sauldre fills the moat of this
fierce-looking 15th-century castle, whose
Renaissance courtyard is more
welcoming. The rooms have 17th-
century furniture and a mechanical spit
stands idle in the kitchen while, in the
chapel wall, a window built 200 years
ago allowed the Princesse de la Trémoille
to 'attend' services without leaving her
room. Recitals and concerts are given
here as part of the July Festival de
Boucard.
40km northeast of Bourges off the D923.
Tel: 48 58 72 81. Open: daily. Closed:
January; Monday, Tuesday in February;
Thursday from March to May and mid-
September to December. Admission charge.

Jacques Migeon, a potter, in his studio at
La Borne

BRIARE-LE-CANAL

The 19th-century engineer, Gustave
Eiffel, is best-known for the Tour Eiffel
in Paris, but his Pont-Canal at Briare is
also a technological wonder. This
aqueduct carries the Canal Latéral across
the Loire to join the Canal de Briare.
Stylish, Parisian-style obelisks serve as
lamp holders, guarding each end of the
bridge, whose 663m-length is the longest
in Europe. Known as the Ruban d'Eau
(Ribbon of Water), the aqueduct took
seven years to build (1890–97) and
finally fulfilled Henri IV's dream of
linking the Mediterranean to the English
Channel using a network of rivers and
canals. Park by the Port de Plaisance
boat marina, on the south side of town,
and walk across the aqueduct to watch
holidaymakers in their *péniches* (holiday
boats) chug past. Like many small towns
in the area, there is a tradition of
enamelling.
75km northeast of Bourges.

LA BUSSIÈRE, CHÂTEAU

Another of the region's more intimate
châteaux, this early 17th-century gem
has acquired the nickname of the
Château des Pêcheurs, the Fishermans'
Castle, because the Chasseval family
owners have collected a mountain of
angling memorabilia, including paintings
and porcelain, rods and flies and even a
stuffed coelacanth. The aquarium of
local freshwater fish makes the collection
even livelier. The château stands on a
little island in a lake and the grounds,
landscaped by Jean le Nôtre, have been
restored, along with the 18th-century
jardin-potager (vegetable garden).
*85km northeast of Bourges on the N7.
Tel: 38 35 93 35. Open: daily, late March
to early November. Closed: Tuesday except
July, August. Admission charge.*

LA CHAPELLE D'ANGILLON

This little known town was the birth place
of Henri Alain-Fournier (real name Henri-
Alban Fournier (1886–1914), son of a
schoolmaster and author of the romantic
and semi-autobiographical novel, *Le Grande
Meaulnes* (1913), known in English as *The
Lost Domain*. He was killed at St Remy
soon after the outbreak of World War I.
Inside the dilapidated exterior of the town's
Château de Béthune (the Comte d'Oigny
is doing his best to restore the 800-year-old
building; the original 15th-century columns
lie in the courtyard, waiting to be re-
erected) is a small museum dedicated to
the author. The chapel, with its Luca della
Robbia *Madonna and Child* is still filled on

A moment of reflection: La Charité-sur-Loire with its 16th-century bridge

a Sunday morning. The Chambre du Roi, where Henri IV and Louis XIV both slept, has a fine painting of St Stephen by Murillo. The Duc de Sully bought the estate 300 years ago because it included the Principality of Boisbelle, which was exempt from all taxes. The current Comte wishes it still were!

32km north of Bourges. Tel: 48 73 41 10. Open: daily. Admission charge.

LA CHARITÉ-SUR-LOIRE

The eccentric name recalls the generous monks who helped pilgrims on their way to and from Santiago de Compostella, in northwest Spain. The abbey church of Nôtre-Dame, consecrated in 1107, was second in size only to that at Cluny and it is still impressive, despite damage from a fire in 1599. The place des Bénédictines, off the Grande Rue, offers a good view of the red-tiled *chevet*, or east end of the church, and the slate-roofed Tour de Bertrange; unfortunately it is too far away to decipher the carvings.

The town has retained its medieval character, so it is worth wandering through the narrow streets to the ramparts overlooking the Loire, spanned by a 16th-century 10-arched bridge. Some houses are gabled, others recycled from the abbey complex. Joan of Arc paid a visit in December, 1429.

52km east of Bourges on the N151.

GIEN

Badly damaged in World War II, much of the rebuilding of Gien has been carried out in an unsympathetic manner, particularly the Centre Anne de Beaujeu, named after Charles VIII's business-like sister, who built the hilltop church, which was reconstructed in brick after 1945. The church itself, dedicated to Joan of Arc, has faïence panels on the outside recording her four visits in 1429. Next door, the colours of the red, black and white brickwork on the castle reflect the proximity of Burgundy, while the lifesize statue of a stag symbolises the Hunting Museum inside. This displays horns, crossbows, stuffed bears and boars and some 70 paintings by Louis XIV's official hunt painter.

Gien is best-known for its high-quality faïence, painted with traditional animal, bird and flower patterns – even the street signs are made of the tin-glazed earthenware, introduced in 1821 by an Englishman. The factory attracts coachloads of visitors who tour the museum and works, then buy from the supermarket-like shop.
Musée de la Faïencerie de Gien, place de la Victoire. Tel: 38 67 00 05. Individuals can join group tours by calling ahead. Museum – open: daily. Admission charge.
Musée International de la Chasse, Château de Gien.
Tel: 38 67 69 69. Open: daily, late February to December. Closed: Monday in winter. Admission charge.

78km northeast of Bourges off the D940.

CHAVIGNOL

This attractive village, wedged between the Sancerre vineyards, is the production centre for one of France's best goat's cheeses, still made to a recipe recorded as early as 1573. The curds from raw goat's milk are moulded, then salted individually. After 12 days, they are known as *bleutés* because of the slightly bluish skin. Left for 20 days, they become *très secs* (very dry). Stored for longer in a crock-pot, they become *repassés* (well-aged). At this point, they are round brown balls, nicknamed *crottins* for their resemblance to horse dung. Gourmets argue the merits of each type – over a glass of Sancerre, of course.
50km northeast of Bourges, just west of Sancerre off the D955.

Gien is famous for its faïence pottery

The grandiose plans for Henrichemont were never completed

HENRICHEMONT

After the Duke de Sully bought his tax haven of La Chapelle d'Angillon (see page 125), he planned to build a Protestant enclave here, named after the king he served (*Henrici mons* means Henry's Hill). Unlike Richelieu (page 76), it was never completed. Today, only the eight streets radiating from the main square of this dull town hint at the 17th-century design.

27km northeast of Bourges off the D940, D11.

MENETOU-SALON

Menetou-Salon is near Sancerre, but has its own *appellation contrôleé* red, white and *rosé* wines. The château was built in 1450 by Jacques Coeur, Charles VII's finance minister (see page 121). The restoration a century ago was inspired by his house in Bourges and paid for by Prince Auguste d'Arenberg, president of the Suez Canal Company. The collection of vintage cars includes an 1899 Panhard Levasseur.

20km northeast of Bourges on the D11. Tel: 48 64 80 16. Open: daily, Easter to October. Closed: Tuesday. Admission charge.

MOROGUES

This commune in the Menetou-Salon wine-growing area boasts the 14th-century Château de Maupas, which deserves a visit. The Maupas family were administrators to the Duchess of Berry and her son, the Comte de Chambord, pretender to the French throne. This explains the souvenirs relating to France's final flirtation with the restoration of the monarchy only a century ago. Surprisingly, there is no local faïence in the 887-piece collection of plates lining the staircase.

25km northeast of Bourges on the D59. Tel: 48 46 41 71. Open: daily, Palm Sunday to mid-November. Admission charge.

Local delicacy: Sablé de Nançay biscuits

NANÇAY

The sophisticated shops here come as a surprise, until you learn that chic Parisians spend weekends in this village. Local author Alain Fournier (see page 124) holidayed here at the turn of the century and the château may have been the setting for the *fête étrange* in his novel, *Le Grande Meaulnes*. Today it houses an arts and crafts gallery, open at weekends. Sablé de Nançay biscuits are the local delicacy, and one of the world's largest radio-telescopes is hidden in the woods.
35km northwest of Bourges on the D944.

NEVERS

Thousands of pilgrims flock to the Convent of St Gildard, northwest of the city. In 1866, Bernadette Soubirous, later St Bernadette, arrived here from Lourdes to join the Sisters of Nevers. She died here in 1879, aged 35; her body is on view in a glass casket. Bernadette was canonised in 1933 and a summer 'musical' based on her life, was inaugurated in 1995.

Like Gien, Nevers is known for faïence, made here since 1648. Although the town museum explains the making of this tin-glazed stoneware, most visitors head for the Bout-du-Monde shop on rue de la Porte-du-Croux (whose workshops are open the first Wednesday of the month).

The city's architectural highlights include the church of St-Etienne, the Porte-du-Croux city gate, the cathedral of St-Cyr-et-Ste-Julitte and the Ducal Palace.
69km southeast of Bourges.

NOIRLAC ABBEY

Even though Noirlac lies just outside the boundaries of this book, the 12th-century white-stone abbey is worth a detour. The restored church, cloisters and chapter house, on the banks of the Cher, were built for the Cistercian order, founded in 1098 to get back to the monastic basics of prayer, austerity and simplicity. Cistercian abbeys, often situated in isolated valleys, had no stained glass, paintings or sculpture. A special exhibition here explains the significance of gestures in medieval miniatures, while the summer concerts are particularly atmospheric.
Bruère-Allichamps, 40km south of Bourges off the A71 motorway. Tel: 48 96 23 64.
Open: daily. Closed: Tuesday, October to January. Admission charge.
Concert details – tel: 48 67 00 18.

POUILLY-SUR-LOIRE

This unremarkable town produces a remarkable wine: Pouilly-Blanc-Fumé (not to be confused with Pouilly-Fuissé in Burgundy). Grapes have been grown here for 1,500 years. The town's current fame dates back to the 19th-century planting of the Sauvignon Blanc variety. The *fumé* (smokiness) supposedly refers to the *pierre-de-fusil* (gunflint) flavour that pundits love. Pale gold in colour, and very dry, Pouilly

Ancient and modern: new stained glass in Nevers' medieval cathedral

wines should be drunk young. White meats and fish are a perfect partner. *57km northeast of Bourges.*

SANCERRE

Downstream from Pouilly, the hilltop town of Sancerre has more character, but experts disagree about the merits of the two wines (like that of Pouilly, Sancerre is also made from the Sauvignon Blanc grape). The ramparts and circular Tour des Fiefs recall the seven-month siege of the Wars of Religion (see pages 58–9). Today, white-stone houses line the streets while the sloping Nouvelle Place is the place to buy arts and crafts, wine, local goat's cheeses and tasty biscuits such as *palettes sancerroises* (with nougat and orange peel).

Rue Macdonald honours another group of Scots; these fled with Bonnie Prince Charlie and settled here in the mid-18th century. Halfway down, a plaque commemorates a descendant, one Alexandre, who became Marshal Macdonald, one of Napoleon's most trusted military leaders. From the Esplanade de la Porte César, there is a sweeping northeasterly view over the Loire. *47km northeast of Bourges.*

Santé! Taste the local vintage on Sancerre's main square

Old Bourges

The heart of Bourges has many fine medieval half-timbered houses. These are being slowly refurbished as local people realise the attractions of living here. *Allow 45 minutes.*

Start in front of the main entrance to the cathedral.

1 CATHÉDRALE DE ST-ÉTIENNE

Spend a few minutes admiring the west front of this 13th-century Gothic building and imagine how vivid the *Last Judgement* carvings must have seemed to the populace of the Middle Ages.
Walk along the north side of the cathedral, turning into the rue des Trois Maillets, past the 13th-century Grange des Dîmes, where tithes were stored. Turn left into the pedestrianised rue Bourbonnoux.

2 RUE BOURBONNOUX

Half-timbered houses dating from the 15th and 16th centuries line the cobbled street. Many, like No 77, are antique shops; others are restaurants and some are private homes. The palette and easel hanging outside No 33 signify that this is an art gallery; opposite, at No 34, the sign of the violin shows that a repairer of musical instruments works here. Look up above no 16: a *trompe l'oeil* painting shows a little girl peering down. The most photographed house is Aux Trois Flûtes, on the corner of rue Joyeuse. On the left, opposite, is the 15th-century Hôtel Lallemant, now the Museum of Decorative Arts.
In place Gordaine, with its outdoor cafés, look to the left, down another medieval street, rue Coursarlon. Exit from the square, turning left on rue Mirebeau.

3 RUE MIREBEAU

Look above the street level boutiques to appreciate the detail of the 15th- and 16th-century houses.
Turn left on rue Pelvoysin.

Local lore: the cake shop was supposedly Jacques Coeur's birthplace

4 RUE PELVOYSIN

A savings bank now occupies the Hôtel Pelvoysin, named after the 16th-century cathedral architect and built at an angle to catch more light. Spot the lion among the many carvings.
Come out on to place Planchat; turn left on to rue du Commerce and right on rue Jacques-Coeur.

5 PLACE JACQUES-COEUR

Place Jacques-Coeur is named after Charles VII's finance minister (see page 121), whose statue stands in the square, looking across to his palatial 15th-century home, Palais Jacques-Coeur. Above the main entrance, small statues of Coeur and his wife lean over as if to greet visitors. Note his coat of arms, which is a play on his name: it contains a heart (*coeur*) and a pilgrim's shell (the symbol of St-Jacques, or St James, of Santiago de Compostella).
Across the square on the right is the

Municipal Theatre. Continue straight on to rue des Armuriers.

6 RUE DES ARMURIERS

Legend has it that Jacques Coeur was born in 1400, in the house on the corner with rue d'Auron, now a *pâtisserie*. In fact, the house dates from the 16th century.
Enter place de la Préfecture.

7 PLACE DE LA PRÉFECTURE

The administrative headquarters of the *département* of Cher occupy the 18th-century building on the right. This was the site of the Ducal Palace of Jean de Berry, where the future King Louis XI was born in 1423. Continue past the imposing offices and fountain into Avenue H Ducrot. On the right, the ancient half-timbered house squashed between its neighbours is not a museum but a private home, complete with television aerial.
Turn left on rue Victor-Hugo, which will take you to the tourist office.

The Upper Loire

'*W*e've seen the châteaux, so we've done the Loire.' Anyone who thinks this has forgotten that there is still the Upper Loire, a region with its own beauty and history.

South of Nevers, on the N81, the ruins of Rozemont castle are a slowly decaying memory of the Hundred Years' War. The Aron river and the Nivernais Canal join the Loire at Decize, where the Promenade des Halles is a splendid 900m-long avenue of ancient plane trees. Further upstream, the Loire meanders to Digoin, with its 15-arch bridge and another confluence of canals. Roanne, dating back to Roman times, was the highest point upstream regularly navigable by boats. Today, this prosperous town is a place of culinary pilgrimage, thanks to Pierre and Michel Troisgros, whose restaurant (Troisgros, in place Gare) is one of France's finest.

Villerest marks the start of the 30km-long, rapid-filled gorges of the Loire. At the Saut de Perron, the rocks have evocative names: the Stairway, the Wolf and the Black Rock. Feurs and Montrond-les-Bains come next in what is a flat, marshy stretch of the river. The delicate blue Fourme d'Ambert cheese, sold in the local markets, comes from the nearby hills.

At Chambles, the Loire is close to St-Étienne, where coal mined centuries ago was floated downstream on rafts made of *sapins* (pine logs). From here the river passes a chain of small towns: Rochebaron with its castle; medieval Beauzac and Retournac, standing high above the river.

La Voûte and Polignac boast castles and Le Puy-en-Velay has a dramatic cathedral, with the Black Virgin at the high altar. The final stretch, up to the source, is a twisting, steep climb towards Mt-Gerbier-de-Jonc, 1,000km from the Atlantic Ocean.

A thousand kilometres brings angling pleasure to many

GETTING AWAY FROM IT ALL

'... through scenes
of vineyard, orchard, meadow-
ground and tilth
Calm waters, gleams of sun, and
breathless trees ... '

WILLIAM WORDSWORTH
Early 19th century

Getting Away From it All

AERIAL VIEWS

The Loire Valley looks breathtaking from the air, especially at dawn in summer when viewed from a hot-air balloon – known in France as a *montgolfière* because it was invented by the Montgolfier brothers. Local tourist offices have further details of balloon flights as well as aeroplane and helicopter trips.

HOT-AIR BALLOONS
Air-Espace
Cicogné. Tel: 47 23 57 64.

Buddy Bombard's Great French Balloon Adventures.
Based in Beaune. Tel: 80 26 63 30.

France Montgolfière
Based in Paris. Tel: (1) 40 60 11 23.

Ombre Chinoise
Chanteloup. Tel: 47 57 20 97.

Loisirs-Accueil d'Indre-et-Loire
38 rue Augustin-Frésnel, Chambray-les-Tours. Tel: 47 48 37 27.

BOAT TRIPS

With hundreds of kilometres of rivers and canals in the region, holidays afloat are popular. Boats are available for hire at the following centres.

Inflation: ballooning over châteaux is a memorable, if expensive, experience

Malicorne-sur-Sarthe: one of many villages that can be explored by boat

On the Sarthe, Mayenne and Oudon rivers

From Château-Gontier:
Tel: 43 70 37 83.
From Sablé-sur-Sarthe and Malicorne:
Tel: 41 95 93 13.
From Grez-Neuville: *Tel: 41 95 68 95.*

On the Loire river

From Montjean:
(hire an old *gabare*, the traditional Loire sailing boat). *Tel: 41 72 81 81.*

On the Erdre river

From Nantes:
Tel: 40 14 51 14; 40 37 02 93; 40 69 29 95 or 40 20 24 50.

On the Sèvre river

From Nantes: *Tel: 40 14 51 14.*

HIKING

The French network of long-distance footpaths is well-organised and well-marked. The national paths are called Grandes Randonnées, or GR, and are numbered for identification. The Fédération Française de la Randonnée Pédestre (FFRP) has drawn up excellent maps and guides called *Topo-Guides*. Local tourist offices can advise on where to hike in their area. The best-known walk across the region is GR3, the Sentier de la Loire (The Loire Path). The main section, from Orléans to Saumur, is some 255km long and links Beaugency and Chambord, Chaumont and Amboise, Vouvray and Tours, Azay-le-Rideau and Chinon.
FFRP – 64 rue de Gergovie, 75014 Paris. Tel: (1) 45 45 31 02.

Gardens and Parks

*T*he Loire Valley is not known for large forests or national parks. Although the Forêt d'Orléans lies to the east, only smaller woodlands now remain of the old royal hunting reserves of Amboise, Chinon and Loches. What the Loire Valley does have, however, is gardens. The art of French gardening was born here in the 16th century, when Italian Renaissance culture influenced not just architecture and interior decoration but also the design of gardens. The 17th century brought the most famous landscape gardener of them all, André Le Nôtre, creator of the gardens at Versailles. Today, the gardens of most of the grand châteaux are open to the public, and so are several private ones, though often for just a few weeks each summer. It is always worth telephoning ahead to see if there are any guided tours, which can make the visit even more enjoyable for amateur botanists.

Angers
The Jardin des Plantes (on the northeastern edge of the city, on place mendès-France) is best known for its English-style gardens and first-class displays of rhododendrons, while the Aboretum Gaston Allard (on rue du Château d'Orgement) is a collection of exotic trees from around the world.
Tel: 41 86 10 10. Open: daily. Free.

Bourges
The Jardin des Prés Fichaux was opened in 1930 and still has a real art deco look about it, thanks to the numerous statues dotted along the paths and among the clipped hedges. The formal gardens behind the cathedral are well-maintained.
Boulevard de la République. Tel: 48 24 75 33. Open: daily. Free.

La Bussière
The 17th-century Château gardens, designed by Le Nôtre, have been re-created; the 18th-century kitchen garden flourishes.
85km northeast of Bourges. Tel: 38 35 93 35. Open: see page 124. Admission charge.

Chamerolles
Perfume is the theme of the Château de Chamerolles and of its geometrical Renaissance garden, where the flowers are planted for their scent.
At Chilleurs-aux-Bois, 30km northeast of Orléans. Tel: 38 39 84 66. Open: daily. Closed: Tuesdays and January. Admission charge.

Chanteloup
Chanteloup has a 44m-high pagoda, but nothing else remains of the splendid Versailles-style château destroyed in 1823. The overgrown gardens are being restored according to the original plans.
2km south of Amboise. Tel: 47 57 20 97. Open: daily, Easter to November. Admission charge.

Châteauneuf-sur-Loire
The 86-hectare park surrounding the remains of the château is another Le Nôtre masterpiece, although it was redesigned in 1821. The best known feature is the 800m-long rhododendron walk, which is in its pomp in late May and early June.
Tel: 38 58 41 18. Open: daily. Free.

New England in old France: American entry in Chaumont's garden festival

Chaumont-sur-Loire
Although the grounds of the château have splendid views over the Loire, the real interest centres around the annual festival, an international challenge to gardeners from all over the world to create a themed garden. These have included a Zen garden, a 'poor man's garden' planted with just three packets of seeds, and even 'forgotten flowers from the past', planted by a group of children from Blois.
Tel: 54 20 98 03 or 54 20 99 22. Open: see page 62. Admission charge.

Chemillé
The Jardin des Plantes Médicinales, in the grounds of the town hall, has over 300 varieties of medicinal herbs and plants, which are at their best between mid-May and mid-October.
30km southwest of Angers. Tel: 41 30 35 17. Free.

Cheverny
Giant sequoias (redwood trees) are among the rarities in the château's 17th-century gardens. These include formal French and wilder 'English' gardens.

65km southwest of Orléans. Tel: 54 79 96 29. Open: see page 99. Admission charge.

Doué-la-Fontaine
In the town nicknamed City of the Roses, for its huge industry, the Jardin des Roses has over 250 varieties. Flowering is at its peak between June and October (see page 33).
40km southeast of Angers. Tel: 41 59 20 49. Open: daily. Free.

La Ferté-St-Aubin
The château garden, with its ancient cypress trees and delightful mixture of islands, water and moats hosts a Spring Festival.
18km south of Orléans. Tel: 38 76 52 72. Open: see page 100. Admission charge.

Maulévrier
The 28-hectare Parc Oriental claims to be the biggest Japanese garden in Europe, complete with temples, bridges, a pagoda and a wooden summer-house.
12km southeast of Cholet. Tel: 41 55 50 14. Open: daily May to September; afternoons only, rest of year. Closed: Mondays from January to 1 May. Admission charge.

Montoire-sur-le-Loir

The Parc Botanique de la Fosse at Fontaine-les-Coteaux is the pride of the family who have introduced thousands of exotic trees and plants since 1751.
50km northeast of Tours. Tel: 54 85 38 68. Open: weekend afternoons; Wednesday to Friday in July and August. Admission charge.

Nogent-sur-Vernisson

Trees are the stars in the 100-year-old Arboretum National des Barres, one of France's finest collections, with 10,000 specimens.
60km east of Orléans. Tel: 38 97 62 21. Open: daily, mid-March to mid-November; Monday and Friday afternoons in winter. Admission charge.

Orléans

The city's Jardin des Plantes is 150 years old and has fine greenhouses and an orangery. The rose-garden and flower beds are beautifully maintained. The peaceful Parc Pasteur, opened in 1927, has neat flower beds, trees and shrubs.
Tel: 58 42 22 22. Open: daily. Free.) Out at Orléans-La-Source, the Parc Floral combines a wildlife park with 30-hectares of roses and dahlias, bulbs and irises. *Tel: 38 63 33 17. Open: daily. Free.)*

Talcy

The well-tended château grounds are undergoing further improvements to the walled garden, kitchen garden and orchards.
40km southwest of Orléans. Tel: 54 81 03 01. Open: daily; closed Tuesday in winter. Admission charge.

Tours

The Jardin Botanique is famous for its magnolia walk and its new hothouses devoted to orchids and passion-flowers. The ginkgo and japonicas are also praised. The Jardin des Prébendes d'Oé were designed in 1857 by the Bülher brothers as a city garden with a pond, bridge, cypress and cedar trees; now the garden is a peaceful haunt.
Tel: 47 21 68 18. Both gardens are open daily. Free.

Ussé

The Château d'Ussé boasts formal gardens designed by Le Nôtre. The terraces and beds are still an elegant tribute to his skill.
40km southwest of Tours. Tel: 47 95 54 05. Open: see page 78. Admission charge.

Valençay

With topiary and real animals, fountains and lawns, the gardens surrounding the Château de Valençay appeal to those interested in garden design.
115km southwest of Orléans. Tel: 54 00 10 66. Open: see page 106. Free.

Vernou-sur-Brenne

The beautifully kept Renaissance gardens surrounding the Château de Jallanges stretch for 7 hectares.
10km northeast of Tours. Tel: 47 52 01 71. Open: daily, March to October. Admission charge.

Villandry

Arguably Villandry is the most famous château garden in France. Designed by Dr Joachim de Carvallo it has ornamental and lovers' gardens, water gardens and the well-known kitchen garden. To appreciate the geometric patterns, stand on the terrace behind the château.
15km west of Tours. Tel: 47 50 02 09. Open: see page 79. Free.

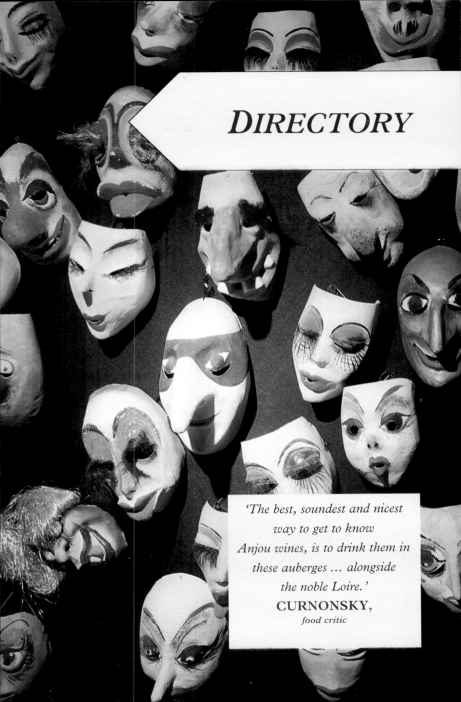

DIRECTORY

'The best, soundest and nicest
way to get to know
Anjou wines, is to drink them in
these auberges ... alongside
the noble Loire.'
CURNONSKY,
food critic

Shopping

*A*s in the rest of France, food is at the top of most shopping lists. Despite the rise of the hypermarket, specialist shops are still an important part of French life.

TYPES OF SHOPS

Boucherie: the butcher's shop, where everything but pork is sold (by tradition, the *charcuterie* – see below – handles pork). Closed Mondays.

Boucherie chevaline: the horse's head outside shows that this is a horse butcher. Open Mondays.

Boulangerie: perhaps the most important shop of all, since the French buy their bread fresh at least twice a day, for lunch and dinner. The long, familiar loaf is a *baguette* but *pain intégral* (wholemeal bread) is common nowadays, as is *pain de campagne*, a heavy white country bread or *pain de seigle*, a slightly sour rye bread, good with cheese. The sign '*dépôt de pain*' denotes shops that sell bread, but do not bake it.

Charcuterie: the *charcutier* once dealt only with the pig and its by-products, such as sausages, terrines and patés. Nowadays the *charcuterie* looks more and more like a delicatessen.

Confiserie: sells sweets made on the premises. Beautifully displayed and wrapped chocolates are always a feature.

Epicerie: literally a spice shop, but nowadays the grocer's, carrying almost everything.

Fromagerie: the best cheese shops are run by *affineurs*, who mature the cheeses they buy from the farmer and sell them at peak condition.

Pâtisserie: cake shops full of home-made tarts and ice-cream, pastries and cakes. Many sell home-made chocolates, too.

Poissonnerie: the best fishmongers often smoke fish and make fish patés and fish soup.

Traiteur: sells ready-made dishes to take home.

Triperie: common in the north of the region, where tripe is a popular delicacy, (it often tastes better when cooked by a specialist).

In the Loire Valley, the high quality of the food shops matches that of the vintners. It is, therefore, the perfect place to indulge the taste buds and discover local specialities.

Amboise

Since 1913, the Pâtisserie Bigot has sold sweet things and offered afternoon tea in an atmospheric old house opposite the entrance to the château.
place du château. Tel: 47 57 04 46.

Country breads in Blois

Tea and cakes, French-style

La Flèche

Another small town where the local specialities are prepared with pride and skill.

Orléans

The *macarons* (macaroons) at Les Musardises are legendary. Find this pâtisserie near the station.
38 rue de la République. Tel: 38 53 30 98.

The Chocolaterie Royale is well over 200 years old. Among the specialities are the *Pralines Jeanne d'Arc*.
2 rue du Tabour. Tel: 38 53 93 43.

Tours

Unusual presentation stops window-shoppers in their tracks outside La Chocolatière, where chocolates come in decorative baskets or pottery dishes.
4 rue Scellerie. Tel: 47 05 66 75.

Angers

At La Petite Marquise, Michel Berrué makes his award-winning *Quernons d'Ardoise*, blue squares of chocolate-coated nougatine that deliberately resemble slates from the local quarry.
22 rue des Lices. Tel: 41 87 43 01.

Bourges

The Cuisine et Vignobles sells both food and wine, and the wines in the cellar are the best of the region.
12 rue Mirebeau. Tel: 48 69 06 59.

La Chartre-sur-le-Loir

This is the sort of 'local shopping' that makes other nationalities feel jealous of the French. Fun to look as well as to buy and try, all round the main square.

Forget factory-produced food: everything at Le Calendos is home-made. Outstanding cheeses, pâtés and wines.
11 rue Colbert. Tel: 47 20 41 20.

Since 1807, Poirault has been an institution for cakes and tea. Ask to watch the sweets being made.
31 rue Nationale. Tel: 47 66 99 99.

Today's specialities at the local butcher

Speciality shopping

The Loire Valley once catered to the tastes of kings and their courts. Those days are long gone but the area can still satisfy even the most dedicated of shoppers. Cities such as Angers, Tours, Orléans and Bourges have a fine assortment of specialist shops, as do the towns of Saumur and Blois. Designer dresses, luxury foodstuffs and antiques shops are often to be found in pedestrianised zones; many stay open until 6 or 7pm. While food shops can be tempting in villages, other shops tend to be less exciting. The exception is Nançay, in the Sologne, where *tout Paris* (the Paris set) goes for weekends and shops for Scottish cashmere, jewellery and art.

Market day in Amboise

Angers

The Maison d'Adam is a tourist site in its own right. Inside, an exhibition centre and shop display the work of local craftsmen and artists.
1 place Ste-Croix. Tel: 41 88 06 27.

La Borne

Potters' workshops are open for visits throughout the summer in and around this hamlet near Henrichemont.
See page 123. Tel: 48 26 73 76.

Bourges

The traditional *mazagran*, a type of elegant mug, is sold in Le Mazagran, along with other local china.
9 rue Bourbonnoux. Tel: 48 69 80 69.

La Coudray-Macouard

Robert Hamon makes *girouettes* (weather vanes). Order one shaped like your own house, or go for the traditional French cockerel.
Atelier de la Girouetterie, rue du Puits-Venier. Tel: 41 67 98 30.

The region is rich with locally made arts and crafts

Mehun-sur-Yèvre
The Centre Régional des Métiers d'Art is a showcase for over 200 painters, potters, jewellers and weavers. *les Grands Moulins. Tel: 48 57 36 84.*

Orléans
Meubles Mailfert, the award-winning manufacturer of reproduction 17th- and 18th-century furniture, is located here in a historic house. *26 rue Notre-Dame de Recouvrance. Tel: 38 62 70 61.*

Poncé-sur-le-Loir
An old mill is now the Centre d'Art et d'Artisanat, a crafts centre, where everything is made and sold on the premises, from pottery to hats and from glass to candles. *On the main road. Tel: 43 44 45 31.*

Tours
The pedestrianised rue Colbert is full of antiques shops but there are also modern craftsman, such as M Bonvallet, whose painted furniture adds a touch of whimsy to bedrooms, bathrooms and even to kitchens. *Forêt Magique, 125 rue Colbert. Tel: 47 64 80 52.*

MARKETS AND FAIRS
This 'garden of France' has abundant markets thanks to the production of luxury fruit and vegetables, such as asparagus and strawberries, plus local wines and cheeses.

Amboise	Wednesday, Friday, Saturday
Angers	daily
Azay-le-Rideau	Wednesday
Beaugency	Saturday
Blois	daily, Saturday morning
Bourges	Tuesday
La Chartre-sur-le-Loir	Thursday
Château-Gontier	Thursday, Saturday morning
Chinon	Thursday, Saturday, Sunday
La Flèche	Wednesday, Sunday
Fontevraud	Wednesday, Saturday morning
Gien	Wednesday, Saturday morning
Langeais	Sunday
Loches	Wednesday, Saturday
Le Lude	Thursday
Montlouis-sur-Loire	Thursday
Montoire-sur-le-Loir	Wednesday
Montrichard	Monday, Friday
Nantes	daily, but best on Saturday
Orléans	Tuesday to Thursday, Saturday
Richelieu	Monday, Friday
Romorantin-Lanthenay	Wednesday, Friday, Saturday
Sablé-sur-Sarthe	Monday, Wednesday
Sancerre	Saturday (all year), Tuesday (in March to November)
Saumur	Saturday, Tuesday to Thursday
Selles-sur-Cher	Thursday
Sully-sur-Loire	Monday
Tours	daily
Valençay	Tuesday
Vendôme	Friday

Villaine-les-Rochers
Basket-weaving has been a speciality since 1849 and the Société Coopérative Agricole de Vannerie is the place for buying hand made souvenirs. *In the village. Tel: 47 45 43 03.*

Wines

*C*hoice is the only problem facing wine lovers in the Loire Valley, which boasts some 60 wine appellations and *Vins Délimités de Qualité Supérieure* (VDQS) areas. These have to satisfy high-quality standards laid down by the national controlling authority. With a wide selection, in all price bands, there is real scope for comparing and contrasting.

MUSCADET
Best drunk young, so avoid any 'bargains' that are over three years old. The best houses include Louis Métaireau, Chéreau-Carré and Donatien Bahuaud.

Maison des Vins de Nantes, Bellevue
44690 La Haye-Fouassière. Tel: 40 36 90 10; fax: 40 36 95 87.

ANJOU AND SAUMUR
Some 25 appellations produce in excess of 11 million cases a year. For an overview, visit the special wine centres in Angers, opposite the castle, and in Saumur, near the army barracks.

Maison des Vins d'Anjou et de Saumur
5 bis, place Kennedy, 49100 Angers. Tel: 41 88 81 13; fax: 41 86 71 84.

Maison du Vin, Saumur
25 rue Beaurepaire, 49400 Saumur. Tel: 41 51 16 40; fax: 41 51 16 14.

Over in the Layon Valley, the Bonnezeaux and Quarts de Chaume are the most prized appellations of the sweet, white Côteaux du Layon wines. At their peak, they match the Sauternes of Bordeaux for quality, while undercutting them in price. Get acquainted with Layon wines at St-Lambert-du-Lattay, 20km south of Angers, where 17 local growers take turns to display (and talk about) their wines.

Maison du Vin
Place du Musée de la Vigne et du Vin, 49750 St-Lambert-du-Lattay. Tel: 41 78 43 84. Open daily in summer.

The main producers of the region's sparkling wines have their headquarters at St-Hilaire-St-Florent, west of Saumur. 'A high-quality alternative to Champagne' says American wine guru Robert Parker of the wines produced at Bouvet-Ladubay, founded in 1851. Equally famous are Ackerman-Laurence and Gratien and Meyer.

Bouvet-Ladubay
1 rue de l'Abbaye, St-Hilaire-St-Florent, 49400 Saumur. Tel: 41 50 11 12. Open daily. They also run a wine-school.

TOURAINE
The red wines of Chinon are very fine indeed, and often compared with a Beaujolais. Producers such as Charles Joguet and Couly-Dutheil are outstanding, turning their Cabernet Franc grapes into complex, spicy, berry-scented wines at competitive prices.

Also underestimated outside France are the still and sparkling white wines of Vouvray, east of Tours. At Gaston Huet's estate, traditional, semi-organic methods are used to produce wines extolled by the novelist Sir Walter Scott in 1827.

Domaine Huet
11–13 rue de la Croix-Brisée, 37210 Vouvray. Tel: 47 52 78 87.

Marc Brédif
Quai de la Loire, 37210 Rochecorbon. Tel: 47 52 50 07.

The Cave des Producteurs brings together 50 wine-growers. The wines are bottled and matured in cellars in 1km of galleries dug into the rock. Free tastings.

Cave des Producteurs
38 La Vallée Coquette, 37210 Vouvray. Tel: 47 52 75 03; fax: 47 52 66 41.

SANCERRE AND POUILLY-FUMÉ
Under pressure from New World wine-makers, the producers of Sancerres have developed a new, cleaner style of wine, well represented by Henri Pellé and Jean-Max Roger. Traditional well-

Dégustation in a wine cellar

structured Sancerres are produced by _vignerons_ such as Vacheron, Paul Cotat and Lucien Crochet.

When it comes to Pouilly-Fumé, on the east bank of the Loire, J C Chatelain, Serge Dagueneau and Baron de Ladoucette, of Château du Nozet, are the star names.

Vacheron et Fils
1 rue du Puits Poulton, 18300 Sancerre. Tel: 48 54 09 93.

OTHER WINES
In the small town of La Chartre-sur-le-Loir, Joël Gigou makes rare Jasnières in both white and red versions.

Joël Gigou
4 rue des Caves, 72340 La Chartre-sur-le-Loir. Tel: 43 44 48 72.

In the Eastern Loire, Menetou-Salon, Quincy and Reuilly are little-known wines, but fine, light and quaffable.

Cultural Events

*W*ith its châteaux, churches and abbeys, the region is rich with ready-made concert halls. Summer festivals abound.

Amboise
The classical music festival is a feature of the town in summer.
Tel: 47 57 09 28. Mid-July to mid-August.

Aubigny-sur-Nère
The Franco-Scottish Festival (see page 122) takes place on the weekend nearest to Bastille Day (14 July) and celebrates the 'Auld Alliance' (going back 700 years) with kilts and bagpipes, parades and dancing.
Tel: 48 81 50 00.

Bourges
The spring festival of French song is a regular feature, while the magnificent organ at Bourges Cathedral is the central theme of a series of summer concerts and exhibitions.
Tel: 48 20 25 24. Mid-July to late August.

Chaumont-sur-Loire, Fougères-sur-Bièvre and Talcy
L'Été des Trois Châteaux (The Summer of the Three Châteaux) presents concerts throughout July and August.
Tel: 54 02 98 03.

Clisson
Baroque and classical music with authentic period instruments in this Italian-style town.
Tel: 40 41 11 27. Last two weeks of July.

Festival finery in Chinon

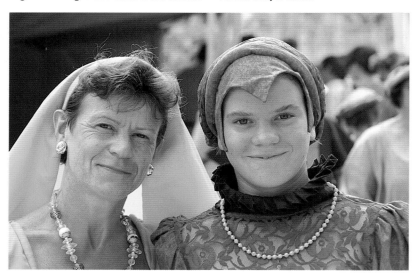

Gargantuan celebrations at Chinon's Rabelaisian medieval market

Cunault
The ancient abbey at Cunault, and the nearby church at Trèves, play host to the annual *Heures Musicales* festival with concerts on Sundays at 5pm in July and August.
Tel: 41 67 92 55.

Doué-la-Fontaine
The City of Roses has a week of flowery festivities each year, called the *Journées de la Rose*.
Tel: 41 59 20 49. Third week of July.

Fontevraud
Classical music concerts are a regular feature at the Royal Abbey (see page 65).
Tel: 41 51 73 52. April to Christmas.

Montoire-sur-le-Loire
The annual international folk festival is now one of France's best.
Tel: 54 72 60 91. Second week of August.

Noirlac Abbey
The summer music festival in the former Cistercian abbey is well established after more than a decade.
Tel: 48 67 00 18. Early July to early August.

Orléans
The 10-day *Fête de Ste-Jeanne d'Arc* commemorates the liberation of the city by the saintly soldier in 1429.
Tel: 38 79 26 47. 26 April to early May.

St-Florent-le-Vieil
The annual music festival only began in the late 1980s, but is already esteemed.
Tel: 42 22 69 51. Mid-June to late July.

Sully-sur-Loire
The château is the focus of an annual festival of music and dance, often with a theme (in 1994 it was 'America').
Tel: 38 36 29 46. Three weeks in late June, early July.

Festivals and Events

FAIRS

February: last weekend: Azay-le-Rideau: wine fair
third weekend: Montlouis-sur-Loire: Wine Fair

March: Thursday before Palm Sunday: Sancerre: old-fashioned market

April: Saumur: wine festival

May: 1 (or next weekend): Sancerre: cheese fair
First week: Orléans: Fête de Jeanne d'Arc
First weekend: Mennetou-sur-Cher: *andouillette* (sausage) fair
Pentecost weekend: Sancerre: wine fair

June: first weekend: Ste-Maure-de-Touraine: cheese fair; Le Coudray-Macouard: village festival

July: 26: St Anne's Day Tours: garlic and basil fair
Third Sunday: Bourgueil: garlic fair
Saumur: Carrousel (Riding Display)

August: Chinon: medieval market
Second week: Montoire-sur-le-Loir: folk festival
Third weekend: Menetou-Salon: open wine cellars
Last Sunday: Sancerre: wine fair

September: first Wednesday: Amboise: melon fair
Second Tuesday: Bourgueil: wine fair

October: About 10: Menetou-Salon: wild mushroom fair
Last weekend: Romorantin-Lanthenay: gastronomic fair
Last Sunday: Sancerre: oyster fair
Last weekend: Azay-le-Rideau: apple fair
Last Tuesday: Bourgueil: chestnut fair

SON ET LUMIÈRE

The sound and light show was 'invented' by P Robert-Houdin in 1952 at Chambord. The idea was to bring the Loire châteaux to life, using recorded voices and lights playing on different parts of the building – a sort of radio drama with spotlights. Since then, it has developed into an art form, often involving hundreds of local people, horses, boats and fireworks. They are an essential part of the Loire Valley experience and a must for every visitor.

Darkness is essential, so most shows start quite late (usually at 10pm), allowing plenty of time for dinner beforehand. Shows are often limited to weekends and holidays. Check by telephone for dates, times, ticket availability and possibility of simultaneous translation in English on headphones. The local tourist office will give helpful tips on parking and so on.

Amboise

Visitors come to *La Cour du Roy François* (the Court of King François I) on Wednesday and Saturday nights to see 420 actors in Renaissance dress. *Tel: 47 57 14 47. Late June to early September.*

Azay-le-Rideau

The interpreter of the story of this moated château is *châtelaine* Philippa Lesbahy. *Puisque de vous, nous n'avons autre visage (As we have no other portrait of you)* is a tour-cum-show with actors in costume.
Tel: 47 31 42 60. Late May to late September.

Beaugency

The town puts on a historical spectacle for a week in summer.
Tel: 38 44 54 42. Late June to early July.

Blois

Ainsi Blois vous est conté (This is the Tale of Blois) at the château is based on a script by Alain Decaux and read by actors such as Robert Hossein.
Tel: 54 78 72 76. Mid-May to mid-September.

Chambord

Les jours et siècles (Days and Centuries) recalls dramatic events in the château's 470-year history.
Tel: 54 20 34 86 or 54 20 31 50. Late April to mid-October.

Chenonceau

Women are the stars in the story of this supremely elegant château, told through a production called *Au Temps des Dames de Chenonceau (In the Time of the Ladies of Chenonceau)*.
Tel: 47 23 90 07. Late May to early September.

Cheverny

This one-hour show at the château is called *Rêve en Sologne (Dreaming in Sologne)*.
Tel: 54 74 06 49 or 54 79 96 29. Mid-July to late August.

Loches

Peau d'Ane (Donkey Skin) is the Charles Perrault fairy-tale about a princess who doesn't want to marry the man selected for her; 130 actors, 250 costumes, horses and fireworks fill the royal castle.
Tel: 47 59 07 98. Early July to late August.

Le Lude

Les Féeries de l'Histoire (Historical Highlights): local history brought to life (see page 150) by local people, using music, horses, boats and fireworks.
Tel: 43 94 62 20. Friday and Saturday in June and July; Thursday, Friday and Saturday in August.

Le Puy-du-Fou

The history of the Vendée region from medieval times to the present day, as seen by a local peasant. Hundreds of actors and 50 horses help to make this France's première *son et lumière*.
Tel: 51 64 11 11. Friday and Saturday night in June and July; and from mid-August to early September.

Meung-sur-Loire

Lewis Carroll's *Alice in Wonderland* visits France.
Tel: 38 44 32 28. Two weeks in the middle of July.

Saumur

Les Tuffolies (Tufa Follies) is an evening show using the château as a backdrop.
Tel: 41 51 03 06. Some 17 performances during July, August and September.

Valençay

La Belle et la Bête, Jean Cocteau's tale of *Beauty and the Beast,* is re-created at Valençay's château.
Tel: 54 00 04 42. Late July to late August.

BRINGING

now playing the lead adult roles.

Le Lude benefits from its setting: spectators park, eat dinner in town and walk to the stands where they look across the river to the gardens and terraces of the château. With no spoken dialogue (the voices are recorded) and only 10 pages of script (available in translation) the plot is easy for foreigners to follow.

When the first *son et lumière* (sound and light) show was organised at Chambord back in 1952, it combined spotlights with taped music and sound effects to tell the story of the château. There were no actors. In 1957, the citizens of the small town of Le Lude in the Loir valley took the idea several steps further and dressed up to re-enact scenes from the Middle Ages and the Hundred Years' War right through to the 19th century. Boats and horses, fireworks and music were set against the background of their château.

What started as a scheme to raise some money for the local school now attracts a total of 50,000 spectators for the 90-minute show, performed on 20 summer nights starting at 10.30pm. Three generations of the community are involved, with the children from 1960

One of France's most spectacular *son et lumière* shows takes place in Le Lude; it includes a lively firework display reflected in the River Loir

CHÂTEAUX TO LIFE

Although the music, such as Beethoven's *Ninth Symphony*, is played by professionals, everyone else is an amateur: in total there are 150 actors, each playing several roles, and 100 'behind-the-scenes' workers, from lighting engineers to programme sellers. The script was written by the town's tax collector. No-one has gone on to be a film star, though a lot of marriages have been celebrated; not surprising, since most of the roles are played by 18- to 25-year-olds who become very good friends as a result of all the rehearsals and performances.

Mistakes do happen, such as the time Mme de Sévigné fell out of her boat or when the royal standard wrapped itself round the messenger's face, temporarily blinding him. Luckily, the horse carried out its moves perfectly. Surprisingly, however, the show has only been rained off twice in 35 years.

Children

'Not another château!' When you hear that cry from the back seat, you know it's time to take a break from castles. Luckily, the past 20 years have seen a real growth in the range of 'things to do' in the Loire Valley. Choose from zoos, underground caves, aquariums and slate mines, as well as a whole host of more traditional museums. Most have reduced rates for children.

Aliotis
From sturgeon to carp, the fish in the Loire and the surrounding rivers are the focus of the Aquarium de Sologne.
Villeherviers, 5km east of Romorantin. Tel: 54 76 07 89. Open: daily. Admission charge.

Amboise
La Maison Enchantée is a house containing 250 automated figures arranged in 25 scenes from history and literature.
7 rue du Général Foy. Tel: 47 23 24 50. Open: daily. Closed: Monday in winter. Admission charge.

The Musée de la Poste includes stage coaches and carriages used by postal services around the world, as well as pictures, letters and stamps.
6 rue Joyeuse. Tel: 47 57 00 11. Open: daily. Closed: Monday and January. Admission charge.

Angers
The Musée de Pignerolle, in the château, is based around the theme of communications – 'from tom-toms to satellites' – and includes a look at the history of electricity and television. Underrated and entertaining.
8km east of Angers. Tel: 41 93 38 38. Open: daily, April to October and Sunday from November to March. Closed: Monday, April to June. Admission charge.

Autrèche
Deer and ugly-looking wild boar are bred in the Domaine de Beaumarchais. Visit in a little train. Boar sausages and venison stews are also sold.
12km north of Amboise. Tel: 47 56 22 30. Open: daily. Closed: Sunday, and Monday from October to March. Admission charge.

Azay-le-Rideau
The Musée Dufresne is packed with 2,000 old cars, tractors, motorcycles and fire engines, some driven by steam, others by petrol engines. A restored paddle-wheel generates power. Picnic areas.
At Marnay, 5km west of Azay. Tel: 47 45 36 18. Open: daily. Closed: January and February. Admission charge.

Blancafort
The region of Berry claims to be the 'sorcery capital of France' and the Musée de la Sorcellerie tells the story of alchemists, elves, magicians and witches in scenes portraying the history and legends of the region.
12km east of Aubigny-sur-Nère. Tel: 48 73 86 11. Open: daily, Easter to October. Admission charge.

Briare
A comprehensive range of vehicles, mainly from the first half of this century, is displayed is in the Musée de l'Automobile.

avenue de Lattre de Tassigny. Tel: 38 31
24 51 or 38 31 20 34. Open: daily.
Admission charge.

Brion

Omlande is an amusement park with
miniature train, a magic river and
regular shows by clowns aimed at
younger children. Picnic areas,
cafeterias.
30km east of Angers. Tel: 41 57 43 19.
Open: daily, June to August; Sunday and
public holidays in April and, May.
Admission charge.

Bué-Bagneux

The Domaine du Menhir specialises in
breeding kangaroos and wallabies as
well as deer, antelopes, donkeys and
llamas. Picnic area, cafeteria.
25km south of Romorantin. Tel: 54 40
62 75. Open: daily, July to September.
Admission charge.

Les Cerqueux-sous-Passavant

Bisonland is a game park where deer and
bison are bred in the grounds of the
Château des Landes. Dried bison, bison
sausages and pâté are also sold.

Old Sun is an Indian chief who acts
as guide to native American customs and
costumes. You can even sleep the night
in a tepee.
25km south of Angers. Tel: 41 59 58 02.
Open: daily, May to mid-September; rest of
year, Sunday and holiday afternoons.
Admission charge.

Châteauneuf-sur-Cher

A wildlife park surrounds the château,
while inside is a display of animated
tableaux illustrating fairy-tales such as
Little Red Riding Hood. Horse displays
are mounted in July and August.
25km south of Bourges. Tel: 48 60 64 21.
Open: daily, April to October; Sunday in
November to March. Admission charge.

Doué-la-Fontaine

The Zoo de Doué, one of the best in
Europe, uses caverns and quarries to
house some 500 endangered species in
near-natural surroundings. Cafeteria.
*17km southwest of Saumur. Tel: 41 59
18 58. Open: daily. Admission charge.*

La Ferrière-de-Flée

'Lilliput' is a doll's museum and
miniature world in the château, with
antique furniture from all over the world.
Good for small children.
*5km from Segré, 40km northwest of Angers.
Tel: 41 92 21 76. Open: weekends and
holidays, May to August. Admission charge.*

La Flèche

In addition to the 800 wild animals, such
as the hippopotamus, giraffe and leopard,
local species are also on view in this zoo,
which also has a museum.
*50km northeast of Angers. Tel: 43 94 04 55.
Open: daily. Admission charge.*

Fresnes

The Château Enchanté de Roujoux
(Magic Castle of Roujoux) is an
amusement park for small children, with
automated figures, dolls, a petting zoo,
play area, animated historic museum,
aviaries and aquariums. Picnic area,
restaurant.
*15km south of Blois, Route de Fougéres. Tel:
54 79 53 55 or 54 79 53 39. Open: daily,
Easter to September. Admission charge.*

Haute-Touche

Rare species, such as the European wolf,
are among the 1,000 animals roaming
freely in the Haute-Touche Wildlife Park.
*3km north of Azay-le-Ferron. Tel: 54 39 20
82. Open: daily, Easter to mid-November.
Admission charge.*

Langeais

The Musée Cadillac is Belgian Robert
Keyaerts' personal collection of Cadillacs:
he has 50 models, including Marlene
Dietrich's 1933 V16 Town Cabriolet.
*At Château de Planchoury, St-Michel-sur-
Loire, 4km west of Langeais. Tel: 47 96 81
52. Open: daily, February to December.
Closed: January and Tuesday in September
to May. Admission charge.*

Mûrs-Erigné

L'Aquarium Tropical has tropical fish
from Asia, Africa and the Americas.
*5km south of Angers. Tel: 41 57 83 14.
Open: daily. Closed: Sunday morning.
Admission charge.*

Noyant-la-Gravoyère

The temperature is a chill 13°C when you
are 130m below ground in La Mine
Bleue, a slate mine with 600m of galleries,
explored by mini-train.
*40km northwest of Angers. Tel: 41 61 55 60.
Open: daily, mid-March to mid-November;
weekends, mid-November to mid-March.
Admission charge.*

Nyoiseau-Châtelais

The Domaine de la Petite Couère is a
vast 80-hectare park, with paths linking

display areas for animals (from llamas to emus), a collection of old farm vehicles, old cars (rather ordinary), old shops (grocers) and homes – all trying to show life as it was a century ago. Quite fun for small children, with room to run free.
Near Segré, 35km northwest of Angers. Tel: 41 61 06 31. Open: Sundays and holidays, April to November; daily, July and August. Closed: Monday. Admission charge.

Renazé

The Musée de l'Ardoise honours the *ardoise* (slate) industry with demonstrations of how slates were mined and made. Audio-visuals in English. Two-hour tour.
50km northwest of Angers. Tel: 43 06 41 74. Open: daily, April to November. Closed: Monday. Admission charge.

St-Aignan-sur-Cher

The Zoo Parc de Beauval has white tigers among its 30 big cats, plus 100 monkeys on an island, 100 snakes and 500 exotic birds in a 9-hectare park. Picnic areas, cafeterias.
35km south of Blois. Tel: 54 75 05 56. Open: daily. Admission charge.

St-Hilaire-St-Florent

An entertaining collection of masks from all over the world, including satirical puppets, are housed in the Musée du Masque.
3km west of Saumur. Tel: 41 50 75 26. Open: daily. Closed: January and, February. Admission charge.

A local factory manufactures masks for export worldwide

Displays by the Cadre Noir, competitions and guided tours of the stables make the Ecole Nationale d'Equitation (National Riding School) a must for fans of the horse (see page 44). *At Terrefort, above St-Hilaire-St-Florent. Tel: 41 50 21 35. Open: daily, April to September. Closed: Sunday, Monday and Saturday afternoons. Admission charge.*

Mushrooms are the subject of the Musée du Champignon, la Houssaye – underground, of course. *Tel: 41 50 31 55. Open: daily mid-Feb to mid-November. Admission charge.*

St-Laurent-des-Autels
The Coulée du Cerf is a wildlife park with 300 animals and plenty of space for running around and enjoying picnics. *10km south of Ancenis. Tel: 40 83 73 25. Open: Easter to mid-November. Admission charge.*

St-Mathurin-sur-Loire
Learn how the Loire River has been controlled over the centuries in the Observatoire de la Vallée d'Anjou, located in a former railway station. *20km east of Angers. Tel: 41 57 08 18. Open: weekends, April to October; daily, July and August. Closed: Monday. Admission charge.*

St-Sylvain-d'Anjou
The precursors of the elegant Loire châteaux are represented here by the reconstructed 12th-century motte-and-bailey Château à Motte in the Parc de la Haie Joulain. *5km northeast of Angers. Tel: 41 76 45 80. Open: daily. Admission charge.*

Saumur
At the Musée des Blindés is one of the world's finest collections of military tanks, many still in working order. *rue Fricotelle. Tel: 41 53 06 99. Open: daily. Admission charge.*

The Musée de l'Ecole de Cavalerie (open daily) and the Musée Equitation et Cavalerie (open July and August) are two museums devoted to the cavalry and its history. *Tel: 41 83 92 99 or 41 51 05 43 (ext 306). Closed: Monday. Identity card required. Admission charge.*

Savonnières
Stalagmites and stalactites, plus 'petrified' sculptures from the 19th century

Iron horses: Saumur's cavalrymen became expert tank drivers

The torture chamber at the Musée Grévin, popular with children

are the highlight of the underground caves, the Grottes Pétrifiantes.
13km west of Tours. Tel: 47 50 00 09. Open: daily, early February to mid-December. Admission charge.

Spay
Some 150 species of exotic birds wander freely in the Jardin des Oiseaux. Picnic areas.
10km south of Le Mans. Tel: 43 21 69 15. Open: daily. Admission charge.

Tours
The Musée du Compagnonnage celebrates the centuries-old guilds of craftsmen. The masterpieces on show range from embroidered white satin slippers dating from 1837 to a gold-medal winner of 1934 – a scale model of Milan's cathedral.

Cloître St-Julien, 8 rue Nationale. Tel: 47 61 07 93. Open: Wednesday to Monday. Admission charge.

The Musée Grévin is one of a chain of waxworks that re-create French history: this deals with Touraine using 31 tableaux and featuring 165 famous personalities.
Château Royal, quai d'Orléans. Tel: 47 61 02 95. Open: see page 57. Admission charge.

Trélazé
The Musée de l'Ardoise is one of several in the region dedicated to the history of slate-quarrying. Good demonstrations.
5km southeast of Angers, 32 rue de la Maraîchére. Tel: 41 69 04 71. Open: Sundays, mid-February to November; daily, July to mid-September. Closed: Monday. Admission charge.

Sport

GOLF

The Loire Valley has many courses, including some quite testing ones. The settings are attractive and some courses are situated in the grounds of a château. For a full list of the ever-growing number of clubs, the French Government Tourist Office has maps and details.

Angers, Golf Club d'

Opened in 1963, this attractive, par-70, 5,460m course has plenty of water hazards.
5km southeast of Angers at Brissac-Quincé. Tel: 41 91 96 56.

Anjou Golf and Country Club

This relatively new complex, designed by Fred Hawtree, has settled well. The 18-hole, par-72 course is one of the longest in the region at 6,250m.
20km north of Angers off the A11. Tel: 41 42 01 01.

Ardrée-Tours Golf Club

A pleasant course in the heart of the country with a château in the background. Giant cedars line the broad fairways; 5,800m, par 72.
12km north of Tours, at Château d'Ardrée, St-Antoine-du-Rocher. Tel: 47 56 77 38.

Les Bordes International Golf Club

Built with money from Baron Bic (of ball point pen and razor fame) and designed by Robert von Hagge, this 18-hole, 6,436m

monster, with a par of 72, is one of France's finest. Superb forest setting. A second 'easier' course has just been built. Echoes of Sawgrass in the USA.
30km southwest of Orléans, at St-Laurent-Nouan. Tel: 54 87 72 13.

Château des Sept Tours Golf Club

Although flat and easy to walk, the architects, Pete and Don Harradine, have used lakes on eight of the holes to test golfers. The course also features some fine old oak trees and stands in the grounds of a 15th-century château; 6,250m, par 72.
35km west of Tours, at Courcelles-de-Touraine. Tel: 47 24 69 75.

Cheverny Golf Club

The Château de Cheverny is the centre-piece for the course (which opened in 1989), a challenging 6,273m long with a par of 71. There is plenty of water to negotiate, and the attractive club house is set in converted farm buildings.
13km south of Blois. Tel: 54 79 24 70.

Cholet Golf Club

A tricky mixture of water hazards and dog legs; 18 holes, par 71, 5,999m.
58km southwest of Angers, near town centre, allée du Chêne Landry. Tel: 41 71 05 01.

L'Epinay Golf Course

Martin Hawtree designed this pleasant 18-hole resort course which, at 5,790m, is not too testing.

GOLF DU CHÂTEAU DE CHEVERNY FRANCE

Golf is one of France's fastest-growing leisure activities

5km northeast of Nantes, near Carquefou.
Take the RN23 towards Angers, then
Carquefou. Tel: 40 52 73 74.

Mans, Golf Club du
In the middle of the 24-hour motor-racing
circuit, with plenty of pine trees and
heather, this is a well-established course;
18 holes, 5,742m, par 71.
Just south of Le Mans, Route de Tours.
Tel: 43 42 00 36.

Nantes-Erdre, Golf de
A quiet, undemanding parkland course
outside Nantes; 18 holes, 6,003m, par 71.
Just northwest of the city on the Rennes road
(RN137). Tel: 40 59 21 21.

Touraine Golf Club
One of the easiest, but also one of the
oldest, courses in the Loire Valley;
5,730m, par 71. The Clubhouse is in the
Château de la Touche.
5km southwest of Tours, near Ballan-Miré.
Tel: 47 53 20 28.

Golf de Marcilly-en-Villette
An 18 hole course, 20km southeast of

Orléans at Domaine de la Plaine.
Tel: 38 76 11 73.

Golf de Sologne
18 holes, 25km south of Orléans, at
Ferté-St-Aubin.
Tel: 38 76 57 33.

Golf du Sancerrois
18 holes at St-Satur, below Sancerre,
47km northeast of Bourges.
Tel: 48 54 11 22.

Golf International des Aisses
25km south of Orléans at Ferté-St-
Aubin.
Tel: 38 64 80 87.

La Baule Golf Course
18 holes, 6127m, par 72. Ten minutes
from La Baule. Domaine de St-Denac.
Tel: 40 60 46 18.

Savenay Golf Course
18 holes, 6335m, par 73. Twenty-five
minutes from Nantes on the RN165,
take the Blain/Bouvron exit.
Tel: 40 56 88 05.

FISHING

The French are mad about both game and coarse fishing. Although different regions have slightly different regulations, there are two basic river categories or classifications. *Première catégorie* rivers, open from about March to September, are for game fishing (trout and salmon); *deuxième catégorie* streams, open almost all year long, are for coarse fishing. In the Loire and its numerous tributaries the main prize is the *brochet* (pike). Also popular are *sandre* (zander or pike-perch), *perche* (perch), *gardon* (roach), *carpe* (carp), *brème* (bream), *goujon* (gudgeon) and *anguille* (eel).

Each *département* issues its own licences (which are mandatory), and this can make life difficult for the casual angler. Fortunately, several hotels and tour operators cater to anglers. Ask for details at your nearest Thomas Cook office. A useful map is *Pêche en France* (*Fishing in France*) prepared by the Conseil Supérieur de la Pêche, 134 avenue de Malakoff, 75016 Paris (tel: (1) 45 01 20 20. Also available at local tourist offices.

CENTRES DE LOISIRS

When children want to stop sightseeing and swim or run free, *centres de loisirs* (leisure parks) are ideal. The following are the bigger ones; more are listed by local tourist offices.

Angers

Parc de Loisirs du Lac de Maine has everything from windsurfers and canoes to tennis and a café.
49 avenue du Lac de Maine. Tel: 41 22 32 10.

Chalonnes-sur-Loire

Les Goulidons is a peaceful setting for fishing, mountain-bike hire, horse-riding and tennis.
20km southwest of Angers. Tel: 41 78 03 58.

Cholet

Centre d'Initiation aux Sports de Plein Air is a busy outdoor centre with camp site, canoes, mountain bikes, horses and tennis.
Port de Ribou, 58km southwest of Angers. Tel: 41 62 12 77.

Couture-sur-le-Loir

The Trois Lacs leisure centre has jet-skis and 4-wheeled bikes.
45km north of Tours. Tel: 54 72 47 59.

Mansigné

A vast stretch of water offers opportunities for sailing, and for riding and biking on the shore; there is also an indoor heated swimming pool which is especially welcome during spring and autumn holidays.
60km northeast of Angers. Tel: 43 46 10 33.

All you need is time, patience, a licence ... and lots of luck

Marçon

The Marçon Centre de Loisirs offers boats and windsurfers for hire, plus tennis and horse riding.
40km northwest of Tours, near Château-du-Loir. Tel: 43 44 13 07.

Noyant-la-Grayère

Parc de Loisirs St-Blaise offers well-supervised swimming, canoes and horseriding, plus a camp site.
36km northwest of Angers. Tel: 41 61 75 39.

La Possonnière

The Arche amusement and leisure park has waterslides as well as pedaloes and swimming.
On the Route de St-Georges-sur-Loire, 15km southwest of Angers. Tel: 41 72 21 09.

Right: families swim in the Vienne
Below: the calm waters of Le Loir are popular with canoeists

Food and Drink

*O*ne of the region's most famous culinary figures is André Curnonsky (1872–1956), the food writer born in Angers. He praised *la mesure* (the moderation) of the Loire Valley cuisine, in which ingredients are allowed 'to taste of what they are.' This 'garden of France', as the 16th-century writer Rabelais called it, produces everything for the kitchen: tender vegetables and fruits; fish from the Loire and nearby Atlantic Ocean; veal, pork and lamb from north of the river; and wild boar, venison, pheasant and wild mushrooms from the Sologne.

Soups are simple: *soupe tourangelle* is based on chicken broth, dotted with the excellent young peas, turnips, leeks and cabbages of the area. *Bouilleture* is a thick soup or stew of freshwater fish with wine; *matelote* is an eel stew using red wine. More delicate are the *quenelles de brochet* (ovals of poached pike mousse).

Among main dishes, one of the best known is *noisettes de porc aux pruneaux de Tours* (pork medallions cooked with prunes), while *fricassée de poulet à l'angevine* combines chicken with onions and mushrooms in white wine and cream.

In summer, a typical dessert could be

Mushrooms growing at the Musée du Champignon, St-Hilaire-St-Florent

crémets (cream, cream cheese and egg beaten together) served with fresh strawberries or raspberries. The most famous dish of the region, however, is

BEURRE BLANC
This is the famous sauce used to accompany fish. Beware: it is not as simple as it looks – patience is the key.

Ingredients
3 shallots, chopped as finely as possible; 3 tablespoons white wine, 3 tablespoons white wine vinegar; 250g unsalted butter; salt and freshly ground black pepper.

Method
Simmer the shallots with the wine and white wine vinegar in a heavy-based pan until well reduced and thick. Allow to cool (this can be done ahead of time). Use a whisk to add the butter, a knob at a time, over a very low heat. The mixture should slowly turn into a thick creamy sauce.

The trick
Take the pan off the heat repeatedly during whisking so the butter does not overheat.

Fresh produce from the 'garden of France'

the legendary *Tarte Tatin* (see page 100), a caramelly apple tart. Purists are shocked by the (delicious) variation that uses pears.

Most of the region's cheeses are made from goat's milk. They are delicious, so don't be put off by the names. The crottin de Chavignol is a small, dry cheese that resembles horse dung (*crottin* in French). Ste-Maure is recognised by the straw threaded through the cheese, while Valençay is pyramidal. The best-known cow's milk cheese is the olivet, from Orléans.

MENU READER

agneau	lamb	*champignons*	mushrooms
ail	garlic	*chèvre*	goat
alose	shad (fish)	*chanterelles*	wild mushrooms
andouilles,		*chevreuil*	venison (technically
andouillettes	sausages made		roe deer)
	from pig's intestines	*chou*	cabbage
	and herbs	*choufleur*	cauliflower
anguille	eel	*crémet or coeurs*	
en matelote	eel stewed in	*à la crème*	a mixture of cream,
	red wine		cream cheese and egg
artichauts	artichokes;		white, often eaten with
à la vinaigrette	cold artichokes with an		fresh berries
	oil and vinegar	*cresson*	cress
	dressing	*Chavignol*	goat's cheese; fresh ones
asperges	asparagus		are served grilled with
barboille,			a salad
poulet en	chicken stew, a Berry	*crottins*	(literally 'horse dung')
	speciality		are an acquired taste.
basilique	basil	*daim*	fallow deer
beurre blanc	white sauce (usually	*darne de saumon*	salmon steak
	served with fish – see	*dinde/*	
	page 163)	*dindonneau*	turkey
biftek	beefsteak	*eau*	water
boeuf	beef	*(gazeuse, plate)*	(sparkling, flat)
boudins blancs	white sausage	*épinards*	spinach
boudins noirs	blood (black pudding)	*escargots*	snails
	sausage	*estragon*	tarragon
bouilleture	fish stewed in red wine	*faisan*	pheasant
broche, à la	on a spit	*farci*	stuffed
brochet		*fenouil*	fennel
(à l'orléanaise)	pike (Orléans-style,	*foie*	liver
	baked with a vinegar	*fonds d'artichauts*	artichoke hearts
	and shallot sauce)	*fouaces*	bread rolls, traditionally
brochette, en	kebab-style		baked in a wood-fired
cailles	quails		oven
canards, canetons	duck, duckling	*four, au*	in the oven
carpe	carp	*fraises*	strawberries
chanciot	Berry speciality of	*framboises*	raspberries
	apple batter dessert	*fricassée de poulet*	
cèpes	boletus mushrooms	*à l'angevine*	chicken, onions and
	(penny buns)		mushrooms simmered in
cerf	red deer (stag)		dry white wine and
cervelle	brains		served with cream

frit	fried	*pintade, pintadeau*	guinea fowl
frites	chips, french-fried potatoes	*porc*	pork
fumé	smoked	*potage (à la tourangelle)*	soup Tours-style with chicken, cabbage, peas, leeks and turnips
girolles	a type of wild mushroom, *chanterelles*	*poulet*	
grenouille	frog	*(à l'Angevine)*	chicken (in a cream sauce with mushrooms, onions and dry white Anjou wine)
haricots	beans		
jambon	ham		
lapin, lapereau	rabbit		
lièvre	hare		
marcassin	young boar	*prune*	plum
marrons	sweet chestnuts	*pruneau*	prune
matelote	fish or eel stew with red wine	*quenelles de brochet*	poached pike dumplings
morilles	wild mushrooms (morels)	*rillettes*	potted meat (usually pork, sometimes goose)
mûres	blackberries	*romarin*	rosemary
myrtilles	blueberries	*sanglier*	wild boar
noisettes de porc aux pruneaux de Tours	pork with prunes	*saucisse*	fresh sausage which has to be cooked, as opposed to *saucisson*, a dried or smoked sausage, ready to eat
nouilles	noodles		
oeufs pochés à la d'Orléans	poached eggs on small chicken tarts with a *sauce suprême* (cream sauce)		
		saumon (à l'oseille)	salmon (with sorrel)
		Selles-sur-Cher	goat's cheese
oie	goose	*steak Curnonsky*	named after the Loire's famous food writer: fillets of beef with beef marrow and grilled tomatoes, port and brandy sauce
Olivet	flat disk of cow's milk cheese from Orléans		
omelette			
(aux fine herbes)	omelettes (with chopped herbs)	*steak à la tourangelle*	fillets of beef with foie-gras-stuffed prunes and Madeira sauce
oseille	sorrel		
perche	perch		
persil	parsley	*Ste-Maure*	cylindrical goats' cheese with straw running through it
petite friture de la Loire	deep-fried assortment of freshwater fish		
		Tarte Tatin	apple tart (see page 100)
pigeon, pigeonneux		*Valençay*	pyramidal goat's cheese
(crapaudine)	pigeon (spatchcocked and grilled)	*veau (cul de)*	veal (rump)
		venaison	venison

RESTAURANTS

The following symbols indicate the price per person of a three-course meal with a half bottle of wine:

F under 100FF
FF 100–150FF
FFF 150–250FF
FFFF over 250FF

ANGERS
Pavillon Paul le Quéré FFFF
A pretty restaurant where chef, Paul le Quéré, uses local wines cleverly in many dishes. Worth it for a special occasion.
3 boulevard Foch. Tel: 41 20 00 20.

Paul le Quéré's elegant restaurant

Angers Les Plantagenêts FFF
A sophisticated setting in the Hôtel de France.
8 place Gare. Tel: 41 88 49 42.

AZAY-LE-RIDEAU
L'Aigle d'Or F
This is the only recommendation in this touristy town. Food is unimaginative but reliable enough.
10 rue A-Riché. Tel: 47 45 24 58.

BLOIS
Le Bocca d'Or F
Well-priced local dishes by Patrice Galland; reasonably priced wines.
15 rue Haute. Tel: 54 78 04 74.

L'Espérance FF
Try to get a table overlooking the Loire. Complex dishes, with fish particularly well-cooked.
189 quai U-Besnard. Tel: 54 78 09 01.

Au Rendez-Vous des Pêcheurs FF
Where the locals go for good value, bistro-style, in a former grocer's shop.
27 rue Foix. Tel: 54 74 67 48.

BOURGES
Philippe Larmat FF
A talented chef with innovative ideas in a courtyard restaurant.
62 bis boulevard Gambetta. Tel: 48 70 79 00.

Le Bourbonnoux FFF
Chic, rather fancy modern cooking.
44 rue Bourbonnoux. Tel: 48 24 14 76.

D'Antan Sancerrois FF
Atmospheric bistro with traditional local dishes.
50 rue Bourbonnoux. Tel: 48 65 96 26.

BRINON-SUR-SAULDRE
La Solognote FF
Dominique Girard's cooking is in tune with the countryside.
Grande-Rue. Tel: 48 58 50 29.

CHENEHUTTE-LES-TUFFEAUX
Le Prieuré FFFF
Jean-Noël Lumineau's food is exquisite enough to distract diners from the panoramic views over the Loire.
Off the D751. Tel: 41 67 90 14.

CHENILLÉ-CHANGÉ
La Table du Meunier FFF
A converted mill on the river where the setting enhances the straightforward food.
In the centre of Chenillé-Changé. Tel: 41 95 10 98.

CHINON
Au Plaisir Gourmand FFF
Uncomplicated dishes served in large portions.
2 rue Parmentier. Tel: 47 93 20 48.

CHOLET
Le Belvédère FF
Chef Inagaki is Japanese but the dishes are French. Pretty setting.
Southeast of Cholet on the D20, by Lake Ribou. Tel: 41 62 14 02.

CLISSON
La Bonne Auberge FF
Amazing things are done with the lobster: delicate desserts.
1 rue O-de-Clisson. Tel: 40 54 01 90.

COURÇAY
La Couture FF
The sort of country inn that visitors look for; situated in a fortified farmhouse.
On the RN 143. Tel: 47 94 16 44.

LA FLECHE
Hôtel du Vert Galant F
Vine-covered inn serving *poule au pot* in honour of Henri IV, whose grave is in the nearby church.
70 Grande Rue. Tel: 43 94 00 51.

FONTEVRAUD
Auberge de l'Abbaye F
Nothing special, but useful for visitors to the abbey.
8 avenue Roches. Tel: 41 51 71 04.

GRAND-PRESSIGNY
L'Espérance FF
Bernard Torset exemplifies the best of Loire Valley cooking with its emphasis on fresh produce, simply prepared.
place Carroir-des-Robins. Tel: 47 94 90 12.

LANGEAIS
Le Langeais FFF
Old-fashioned quality, set below the castle.
2 rue Gambetta. Tel: 47 96 70 63.

LOCHES
Le George-Sand FFF
Below the ramparts of the château; competent.
39 rue Quintefol. Tel: 47 59 39 74.

LOUDUN
La Reine Blanche FF
Pascal Meiche seems to get better and better. Well-priced.
6 place Boeuffeterie. Tel: 49 98 51 42.

LUYNES
Domaine de Beauvois FFFF
Elegant dining in a château overlooking countryside.
D49, 4km northwest. Tel: 47 55 50 11.

MONTBAZON
Château d'Artigny FFFF
One of the most splendid hotel dining-rooms in the region. Up-market and expensive.
Rte d'Azay-le-Rideau. Tel: 47 26 24 24.

MONTBAZON
La Chancelière FFFF
The affluent citizens of Tours come to
this elegant old house when they want to
celebrate.
1 place Marronniers Tel: 47 26 00 67.

NANTES
Villa Mon Rêve FF
Stylish food and a pretty garden on the
south bank of the Loire.
*7km east of Nantes at Basse-Goulaine on the
Route des Bords-de-Loire. Tel: 40 03 5 50.*

NUAILLÉ
Relais des Biches FF
A good place to try the *sandre* in red-wine
sauce.
place Eglise. Tel: 41 62 38 99.

ONZAIN
Domaine des Hauts de Loire FFF
Rémy Giraud is a superb chef and his
restaurant enjoys a superb setting. Fans
say the experience is worth every centime.
Route d'Herbault. Tel: 54 20 72 57.

ORLÉANS
L'Ambroisie FF
Imaginative cooking near the cathedral.
222 rue Bourgogne. Tel: 38 68 13 33.

L'Archange FF
Alain Schmitt works miracles with fish.
*66 rue Faubourg-Madeleine.
Tel: 38 88 64 20.*

Orléans La Chancellerie FFF
An efficient brasserie on main square,
overlooking the statue of Joan of Arc.
27 place du Martroi. Tel: 38 53 57 54.

PETIT-PRESSIGNY
La Promenade FF
Remarkably well-priced roadside bistro

that is a dream of France come true.
On the D103. Tel: 47 94 93 52.

ROCHECORBON
L'Oubliette FFF
Classy cooking in a troglodyte cave.
34 rue Clouets. Tel: 47 52 50 49.

ROMORANTIN-LANTHENAY
Hôtel d'Orléans F
By contrast to the town's over-priced Lion
d'Or, this small restaurant is a bargain.
2 place Général de Gaulle. Tel: 54 76 01 65.

LES ROSIERS-SUR-LOIRE
Auberge Jeanne-de-Laval FFFF
Old-fashioned and proud of it; excellent
wines.
54 rue Nationale. Tel: 41 51 80 17.

ST-HILAIRE-ST-FLORENT
Le Clos des Bénédictines FFF
Fine views over the city; well-prepared
dishes.
On the D751. Tel: 41 67 28 48.

SAUMUR
Les Chandelles F
Stick to traditional, local dishes; prices
are a bargain.
71 rue St-Nicolas. Tel: 41 67 20 40.

L'Orangeraie FF
At the foot of the château drawbridge.
Tel: 41 67 12 88.

SELLES-SUR-CHER
Le Lion d'Or FF
Old-fashioned riverside restaurant.
14 place Plaix. Tel: 54 97 40 83.

SOUVIGNY-EN-SOLOGNE
La Croix Blanche FF
Village inn with plenty of atmosphere.
rue la Biche. Tel: 54 88 40 08.

La Perdrix Rouge FF
Jean-Noël Beurienne is famous for his
seasonal Sologne game dishes, but is
excellent all year round.
rue Gâtinais. Tel: 54 88 41 05.

THOUARCÉ
Le Relais de Bonnezeaux FF
A converted railway station, serving
delicate dishes and Layon wines.
Route Angers. Tel: 41 54 08 33.

TOURS
Jean Bardet FFFF
Arguably the finest restaurant in the
region, with prices to match. Immaculate
service.
57 rue Groison. Tel: 47 41 41 11.

Barrier FFFF
The grand old man of Tour's cuisine.
101 avenue Tranchée. Tel: 47 54 20 39.

Le Relais des Cigognes FF
On an atmospheric, if touristy, old square.
2 place Plumereau. Tel: 47 20 57 57.

Sunday lunch: La Croix Blanche, Souvigny

Château de Beaulieu FFF
Modern French cuisine at its best.
Elegant hotel dining-room.
*5km southwest of Tours, at Joué-lès-Tours,
on the Route de l'Epend. Tel: 47 53 20 26.*

VENDOME
La Cloche Rouge FF
Up-and-coming restaurant; one to watch.
15 faubourg Chartrain. Tel: 54 77 02 88.

VIERZON
La Grange des Epinettes FF
Big helpings in the most popular
restaurant in town.
40 rue Epinettes. Tel: 48 71 68 81.

**Vignoux-sur-Barangeon Le Prieuré
FFF**
Serious fish cookery off the beaten track.
*Route St-Laurent, on the D30.
Tel: 48 51 58 80.*

VOUVRAY
La Cave Martin F
A chance to eat honest rustic dishes in a
real cave.
66 la Vallée Coquette. Tel: 47 52 62 18.

LOIRE VALLEY WINES

The sheer diversity of Loire wines comes as a surprise to many visitors. The choice includes red, white and *rosé*, dry, medium and sweet, and even *pétillant* and sparkling. In general, however, the wines are light and seem to travel poorly; the best are kept 'at home', and are often served by the glass (12cl), the *fillette* (a pitcher of 25cl) or the *chopine* (50cl).

Muscadet
Made from the Melon de Bourgogne grape, this is the standard accompaniment to a platter of *fruits de mer*. The better Muscadets are from Sèvre-et-Maine, labelled *sur lie*, meaning that the pressed juice is left throughout the winter on the lees in the vat before bottling in the spring: this gives a fuller flavour and adds zing to this light, straw-coloured and acidic wine.

From the same area, around Nantes, the Folle Blanche grape is used to make the very acidic Gros Plant white wine.

Anjou and Saumur
Anjou is best known internationally for the mass-market sales of its sweetish pink Anjou Rosé. Wine experts, however, rave about the dry white Savennières, made just west of Angers from Chenin Blanc grapes, which are at their best after a decade in the bottle. Challenging Champagne in popularity are the sparkling Saumur *brut* (dry) sparkling wines, some even owned by Champagne houses.

The Cabernet Franc grape is grown for light quaffable red wines, such as Saumur Rouge and Saumur-Champigny, often drunk chilled in summer.

Touraine
The Cabernet Franc seems to have more character and depth of flavour further upstream around Chinon, Bourgeuil and St-Nicholas-de-Bourgeuil. When allowed to mature, their complexity approaches that of fine Burgundies.

Around Vouvray and Montlouis, the Chenin Blanc grape is transformed into classy dry, *demi-sec* (medium dry), sweet and *mousseux* (sparkling) white wines. When it comes to value for money, try the refreshing Sauvignon de Touraine, a clean-

Variety plus quality means Loire Valley wines suit all palates

of the Coteaux-du-Layon. On the Loir, locals are fiercely proud of their unusual Jasnières (pronounced Jannyair). Near Bourges, the Sauvignon Blanc and Pinot Gris grapes make Quincy, Reuilly and Menetou-Salon wines; these dry whites and light reds are less expensive than similar Sancerres.

tasting white wine that is a particular pleasure to drink in summer.

Sancerre and Pouilly-Fumé
Until New Zealand came along, nowhere in the world produced finer Sauvignon Blanc wines than the eastern extremes of the Loire vineyards, with their leafy freshness and elegant balance.

Other wines
Hidden away in the Layon Valley are the well-priced, dessert wines

Above: Vouvray wines can be still or sparkling, sweet or dry
Left: Sancerre's wines reflect the flinty soil of the vineyards

UNDERGROUND ATTRACTIONS

Many of the caves of the region, once excavated for their stone, have been recycled as wine cellars and mushroom farms. The most interesting are now restaurants and museums.

Le Coudray-Macouard

The Magnanerie du Coudray is a silkworm farm (the caterpillars grow between May and October) featuring an explanation of silk as a textile. *Impasse de Bel-Air. Tel: 41 67 91 24. Admission charge.*

Dénezé-sous-Doué

Hundreds of sculpted figures and faces are carved in the living rock, supposedly by 16th-century stonemasons evading persecution.

Vouvray wines are stored in caves

Tel: 41 59 15 40. Open: daily, Easter to mid-November. Wednesday, musical evening. Admission charge.

La Fosse-Forges

A complete hamlet has been restored to allow visitors to imagine what daily life would have been like underground. *Tel: 41 59 00 32. Open: daily in season. Admission charge.*

Grézillé

The Clos des Roches is a carefully restored home, complete with bread oven, now used to make *fouaces* (hot bread) for the restaurant. *At Bourgneuf. Tel: 41 45 59 36. Reservation essential.*

Louresse-Rochemenier

The troglodyte village has some 20 rooms, furnished as they would have

been at the turn of the century. There is even a subterranean chapel.
Tel: 41 59 18 15. Open: daily in summer and at weekends spring and autumn. Admission charge.

The **Caves de la Genevraie** is an underground restaurant specialising in *fouaces* (hot bread, baked in a wood-fired oven).
Tel: 41 59 34 22. Open: Friday, Saturday and Sunday in general; longer in high season. Reservation essential.

Montsoreau
The Champignonnière at Saut-aux-Loups gives visitors the story of mushrooms, from cultivation to cooking pot. Afterwards, eat *galipettes* (big caps) stuffed and baked in a stone oven.
Tel: 41 51 70 30. Open: daily.

Parnay
The Château de Marconnay is one of the only troglodyte castles in the Loire region. Taste and buy wines in the cellars.
Tel: 41 67 24 14. Open: daily, April to September. Closed: Monday.

Rochecorbon
Les Hautes Roches is both a restaurant with super views over the Loire and an elegant hotel with rooms in the rock.
Tel: 47 52 88 88. Booking essential. Expensive.

St-Georges-des-Sept-Voies
The Orbière is an underground sculpture by Jacques Warminski that has to be seen to be believed. Visitors tour the inside of this truly unique work of art, chiselled out of 90-million-year-old rock.
Tel: 41 57 95 92. Open: daily. Admission charge.

St-Hilaire-St-Florent
A tour of the mushroom museum is delightfully cool on a hot day.
Route de Gennes. Tel: 41 50 31 55. Open: daily, mid-February to mid-November.

Dark secrets: troglodytic mushrooms

Turquant
The 15th-century windmill, with its grindstones in a cave below the mill, stands alongside a troglodyte farm.
Tel: 41 51 75 22. Open: daily, May to October; weekends in winter. Admission charge.

At the **Troglo'Tap**, apples are dried and preserved as they were centuries ago. A chance to watch – then eat.
Tel: 41 51 48 30. Open: weekends, March to November; daily, June to September. Closed Monday. Admission charge.

Vouvray
La Cave Martin serves regional dishes in a cave in the cliffs.
In hamlet of La Vallée Coquette. Tel: 47 52 62 18. Booking essential. Mid-price.

Stay underground
The central *gîtes* agency for Maine-et-Loire has several *troglogîtes* – self-catering underground homes – on its books.
Tel: 41 23 51 23.

Hotels and Accommodation

*V*isitors are nothing new in the Loire Valley. Back in 1539, Charles V of Spain was the guest of François I at Chambord. Today, you don't have to be royalty to stay in a château; many have been transformed into hotels, ranging from the grand Château d'Artigny near Tours to the smaller Château de Beaulieu at Joué-lès-Tours. There are also old inns, such as the Cheval Rouge at Villandry, and the burgeoning *chambres d'hôtes* (bed and breakfasts). Unless you are travelling during July, August and early September, it is rarely difficult to find a room at the price and standard you require. During the summer holidays, however, advance reservations are essential.

THE STAR-RATING SYSTEM

There are five grades of hotels in France: one-, two-, three- and four-star, and the four-star *luxe* (luxury) category. These stars reflect the range of facilities rather than quality, so a comfortable and friendly two-star hotel may be more to your liking than a more formal four-star hotel which has porters, receptionists and a swimming pool.

The French Government Tourist Office (often known as La Maison de la France) has branches all over the world, where full listings of hotels in the Loire Valley are available, as well as suggestions on how to book ahead. Their annual magazine, *The Traveller in France Reference Guide*, published in Britain, has hundreds of hotel listings, along with reservation numbers. Among the most widespread and popular hotel associations are:

Logis de France: this consists of some 4,000 family-run hotels, mainly in the one- and two-star category. Members are listed in a book, entitled *Logis de France*, that is published annually in March.
Tel: (0171) 493 3480 (UK); (1) 45 84 70 00 (France).

Château-Hôtels Indépendants et Hostelleries d'Atmosphère: over 400 independent, comfortable hotels with a special ambience.
Tel: (1) 43 54 74 99 (France).

Relais & Châteaux: 150 luxury hotels, often in old castles or country mansions.
Tel: (1) 45 72 90 00 (France).

Campanile: 350 modern, motel-style hotels across France.
Tel: (0181) 569 6969 (UK); (1) 64 62 46 46 (France).

Climat de France and **Inter-Hôtel**: 315 two- and three-star hotels, all modern, right across France.
Tel: (0171) 287 3181 (UK); (1) 42 06 46 46 (France).

Le bed-and-breakfast is booming

Ibis and Arcade: 400 modern hotels at two-star level, all over France.
Tel: 0171 724 1000 (UK); 60 77 27 27 (France).

Formule 1: The ultimate economy hotel. Plain, cheap and clean.
Tel: (1) 43 04 01 00 (France).

Once in France, it is well worth stopping at an Office de Tourisme or Syndicat d'Initiative (tourist office) for further suggestions. Some will even be able to offer assistance with your reservations.

SELF-CATERING
Thousands of French and foreign visitors prefer to rent a cottage and cater for themselves. Select the one that suits. The nation-wide Gites de France organisation lists all the available properties in a thick, yellow book.

It is vital to book several months in advance since the main holiday periods are quickly booked up.
Tel: (0171) 493 3480 (UK); (1) 47 42 20 20 (France).

Seal of approval: hotel signs in the Sologne

THOMAS COOK
Travellers who purchase their travel tickets from a Thomas Cook network location are entitled to use the services of any other Thomas Cook network location, free of charge, to make hotel reservations.

Hotels with Character

Auberge du Centre, Chitenay

'Tradition et Terroir'

The motto of France's Logis de France organisation, representing small family-run inns, emphasises that their objectives are to combine tradition with regional character. In the early 1990s, higher standards were set to guarantee greater quality. At Chitenay, south of Orléans, the Auberge du Centre is an excellent example. Here Gilles Martinet works *au piano* (at the piano – meaning the stove) while his wife, Brigitte, ensures guests are warmly welcomed. 'My grandparents began by serving lunch in the kitchen in 1951; now there are telephones and TVs in the bedrooms,' says Gilles who was born here, 'but no mini-bars. I think that is anti-social.' Order specialities like *lapin albicoco* (rabbit with apricots); rent bikes to explore the countryside.
Auberge du Centre, place de l'Eglise, Chitenay. Tel: 54 70 42 11.

At home in a château

Not every château is open to the public – some are just homes. At Les Briottières, north of Angers near Champigné, the de Valbray family were one of the first to offer up-market bed-and-breakfast as a means of paying the maintenance on their 30-room château. Staying here is more akin to being a paying guest at a country estate. 'Most guests come to relax after 'doing' the Loire châteaux. They want to do nothing. They also have the estate and the swimming-pool. We're deep in the country' says the owner, François de Valbray. Each bedroom is furnished with family antiques and equipped with modern bathrooms. The 18th-century mansion has elegant salons to read and chat in, 'but we don't always have dinner with guests. They can chose to be together round a large table or at separate tables – even on the terrace in summer.' Informality is the key word, for this remains a family home, not a hotel, and there are no staff.
Les Briottières, Champigné.
Tel: 41 42 00 02.

Living like a lord

The luxurious 17th-century Château de Noirieux, at Briollay, north of Angers,

Seventeenth-century Château de Noirieux – luxury accommodation at Briollay

has a Michelin-starred chef and atmospheric beamed bedrooms (equipped with satellite TV, mini-bars and marble bathrooms). 'Service is our strength,' says Gérard Come, who even took one guest fishing himself 'because we make that extra effort.' The idea is to offer the best of both worlds, 'a touch of history with contemporary comfort. We have our own chapel, but we also have a swimming pool where guests sip drinks in their deckchairs.' M Come's oriental-style *croustillant de langoustines* is typical of his eclectic cooking style, but the chocolate gâteau, with its liquid-

chocolate centre, is a pure French treasure.
Château de Noirieux, Briollay. Tel: 41 42 50 05.

Messing about on the river

The numerous rivers and canals of the Loire region are all well-served with marinas where you can hire a *péniche*, a houseboat-like holiday boat. No permits are needed and a short on-the-spot lesson by the *loueur* (boat hire company) is enough to get you started. With beds, showers, kitchens and toilets, these may look like floating caravans, but they are spacious enough to accommodate from two to 16 guests (see also pages 134–5.)

On Business

*T*he French are conservative in their approach to business, especially outside the major cities. Allow plenty of time for appointments and do not expect a swift response to your proposals.

The French like to catch up on their paperwork first thing in the morning and have a proper lunch, so the best time for an appointment is mid-morning or mid-afternoon.

Doing business over lunch may be accepted practice in some parts of the world, but in France, meals are considered a social pleasure. You can use these occasions for building friendships, however, and for establishing a stronger client/customer relationship. Never broach business until the coffee stage of a meal, if at all.

There has been a dramatic jump in the number of French who speak a foreign language (usually English). However, just as in any country, the host is always flattered to be addressed in his or her native tongue. Intricate business dealings could well merit the use of an interpreter if the subtleties are not to be lost in translation. All documents should be in French, using the best translators available. The French are sticklers for the letter of the law.

At the same time, the younger French have a more dynamic appraoch to business, especially business-school educated managers working for multi-

France's banking is international

national companies. Some are still keen to have *le power* breakfast, though most think of this as a passing fad.

Meeting and greeting

The formality of shaking hands is very important. See a group of farmers meet at the market and everyone shakes hands with everyone else. The same applies in an office; it is better to shake every hand on arrival and departure. Always dress formally (suit and tie for men and a suit for women). The French judge a person by the way he or she dresses.

The working day

The two-hour lunch hour is standard throughout France, so days are quite long.

Offices are open 8am–12.30pm and 2.30–5pm. Banks are open 9am–noon and 1.30–4.30pm (they also close at noon on the day before an offical holiday). Government offices are open 9am–noon and 2–6pm.

Telefax, fax machines

Fax machines are commonplace in France. Most hotels, even restaurants, have them so confirmation of bookings is much simpler and more reliable.

Minitel

This is a computer keyboard and terminal that hooks into the telephone allowing access to thousands of facts and figures, from share prices to the telephone directory. Many French actually make theatre bookings and pay their bills using Minitel, a considerable technological innovation.

Conventions and seminars

The Loire Valley, so close to Paris by TGV, has a growing reputation for congress and seminar facilities. One of the newest is the startlingly modern Vinci International Convention Centre in Tours, opened in 1993. Local tourist offices have full details.

Conferences and incentive travel are well catered for with specialist offices in each *département*.

Pays de la Loire

CDT Pays de la Loire, 2 rue de la Loire, 44200 Nantes. Tel: 40 48 24 20 or 40 47 11 45; fax: 40 08 07 10.

Centre-Val-de-Loire

CDT Centre-Val-de-Loire, 9 rue St-Pierre-Lentin, 45041 Orléans. Tel: 38 54 95 42; fax: 38 54 95 46.

Practical Guide

CONTENTS

ARRIVING

European Union (EU) residents visiting France need only a passport to enter the country. Citizens of the USA, Canada, New Zealand and most other western European nations need no visa unless they intend to stay for more than three months. Australian and South African visitors need a visa, irrespective of the length of their stay. If you hold a non-EU passport, check entry requirements with your nearest French consulate.

Travellers who require visas should obtain them in their country of residence, as it may prove difficult to obtain them elsewhere. Several types of visa are available – allow plenty of time to apply (two months is advisable).

By air
The region has two main airports with international connections: Nantes and Tours.

By train
The Loire Valley is well served by the French rail system SNCF (Société Nationale des Chemins de Fer), with fast links to Paris. The *Thomas Cook European Timetable*, (published monthly) gives up-to-date details of European rail services (and many shipping services) and will help you plan a rail journey to, from and around France. The timetable is available in the UK from some railway stations and any branch of Thomas Cook, or by phoning (01733) 268943. In the USA, contact the Forsyth Travel Library Inc, 9154 West 57th St (PO Box 2975), Shawnee Mission, Kansas 66201 (tel: (800) 367 7982 – toll-free within US only or tel: (913) 384 3440).

By ferry
There are numerous cross-Channel ferry services linking France to the UK: the nearest French ferry ports are St Malo (for the westernmost Loire Valley), Cherbourg, Ouistreham, Le Havre and Dieppe. These ports are served by Brittany Ferries, Stena Sealink and P&O. Irish Ferries have daily sailings in summer from Rosslare and Cork to Le Havre and Cherbourg.

By road

The *autoroutes* speed visitors through the Loire Valley, from Le Mans via Angers to Nantes (A11), from Paris to Orléans and Tours (A10), and from Orléans to Bourges (A71). The amount of toll payable depends on distance travelled.

CAMPING AND CARAVANNING

The region has many fine campsites, each graded by the tourist boards who rate the number of facilities on offer, from one- to four-star. The French love the great outdoors and almost every village has its camping site.

For more detailed information contact local tourist offices or: Fédération Française de Camping et de Caravanning, 78 Rue de Rivoli, 75004 Paris. Tel: (1) 42 72 84 08.

When travelling by road, vehicles towing caravans must keep at least 50m from other vehicles, have specially extended rear-view mirrors and be no more than 11m in length and 2.5m in width.

CHILDREN

With their large families, children are a natural and welcome part of any holiday in France. Most can sleep in their parent's bedroom for free or for a low supplementary charge. They are welcome in restaurants, many of which offer children's menus and highchairs. Only the grandest restaurants will turn a hair at the sight of a family invasion. When travelling by train, ask for discounts: children under four travel free; from four to 12, they go at half-price.

They call it *le camping*

CLIMATE

The nickname of the 'garden of France' is due to a combination of fertile soil and a mild climate. As soon as visitors driving south from the coast enter the Loire Valley, they notice a distinct lift in temperature. Frost and snow are rarities, but July and August can be quite humid, with temperatures in the high 20s. For most of the year, the pleasantly mild temperatures make this an ideal area for touring and for holidays (as well as for growing grapes).

WEATHER CONVERSION CHART
25.4mm = 1 inch
°F = 1.8 × °C + 32

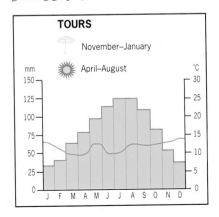

TOURS

November–January

mm   April–August   °C

150 — — 30

125 — — 25

100 — — 20

75 — — 15

50 — — 10

25 — — 5

0 — — 0

J F M A M J J A S O N D

Conversion Table

FROM	TO	MULTIPLY BY
Inches	Centimetres	2.54
Feet	Metres	0.3048
Yards	Metres	0.9144
Miles	Kilometres	1.6090
Acres	Hectares	0.4047
Gallons	Litres	4.5460
Ounces	Grams	28.35
Pounds	Grams	453.6
Pounds	Kilograms	0.4536
Tons	Tonnes	1.0160

To convert back, for example from centimetres to inches, divide by the number in the the third column.

Men's Suits

UK		36	38	40	42	44	46	48
Rest of Europe	46	48	50	52	54	56	58
US		36	38	40	42	44	46	48

Dress Sizes

UK		8	10	12	14	16	18
France		36	38	40	42	44	46
Italy		38	40	42	44	46	48
Rest of Europe		34	36	38	40	42	44
US		6	8	10	12	14	16

Men's Shirts

UK	14	14.5	15	15.5	16	16.5	17
Rest of Europe	36	37	38	39/40	41	42	43
US	14	14.5	15	15.5	16	16.5	17

Men's Shoes

UK		7	7.5	8.5	9.5	10.5	11
Rest of Europe	41	42	43	44	45	46
US		8	8.5	9.5	10.5	11.5	12

Women's Shoes

UK	4.5	5	5.5	6	6.5	7
Rest of Europe	38	38	39	39	40	41
US	6	6.5	7	7.5	8	8.5

CONVERSION TABLES

See opposite.

CRIME

The Loire Valley is quiet and crime-free, but never offer the temptation of visible valuables in the car. At the height of the season, handbags are always at risk in crowds.

DRIVING

Driving licences from all European Union member countries are valid in France, as are American, Canadian, Australian and New Zealand licences. Drivers should always carry the vehicle's registration documents and valid insurance papers. The so-called 'green card', the International Insurance Certificate, is also highly recommended, as is membership of a home-based breakdown/accident recovery scheme.

Road signs are international. Although *priorité à droite* (priority for cars approaching from the right) still applies in built-up areas, the rule no longer applies on roundabouts. If an oncoming car flashes its headlights, it is indicating that it has priority! Dipped headlights should be used in poor visibility, and, of course, at night. Right-hand-drive vehicles should have their headlights adjusted, or use patches to prevent dazzle, though yellow tinting is no longer a requirement. If seat belts are fitted, their use is compulsory, as are helmets for motorcyclists.

Car rental is easy in the region, with all the major international companies represented in the bigger towns; Citer is a reliable French company.

Speed limits

Urban areas: 65kph
Within city areas: 50kph

Single carriageway roads: 90kph (on wet roads 80kph)
Dual carriageway roads: 110kph (on wet roads 100kph)
Motorways: 130kph (on wet roads 110kph); note that a minimum speed of 80kph applies when overtaking in the middle lane.
Motorcycles of less than 80cc have a 75kph speed limit.

Road signs
Rappel is a reminder that speed limit restrictions continue.
Blue signs indicate motorways.
Green signs indicate main roads.
White signs indicate local roads.
Green signs with *bis* in yellow are alternative quieter routes.
Yellow signs indicate a *déviation* (diversion).
Péage: toll; *Ralentir*: slow; *Sens unique*: one-way street

ELECTRICITY
220 volts 50-cycle AC is the national standard along with two-pin continental-style plugs. Adaptors are well worth buying before leaving home.

EMBASSIES AND CONSULATES
Australia: 4 rue Jèan-Rey, Paris 75015. Tel: (1) 40 59 33 00 or 45 75 62 00.
Canada: 35 avenue Montaigne, Paris 75008. Tel: (1) 47 23 01 01.
Ireland: 4 rue Rude, Paris 75016. Tel: (1) 45 00 20 87.
New Zealand: 7ter, rue Léonard de Vinci, Paris 75016. Tel: (1) 45 00 24 11.
UK: 35 rue du Faubourg-St-Honoré, Paris 75008. Tel: (1) 42 66 91 42.
USA: 2 avenue Gabriel, Paris 75382. Tel: (1) 42 96 12 02.

Follow the signs

EMERGENCY TELEPHONE NUMBERS
The Thomas Cook Worldwide Customer Promise offers free emergency assistance at any Thomas Cook Network location to travellers who have purchased their travel tickets at a Thomas Cook location. In addition, any MasterCard cardholder may use any Thomas Cook Network location to report the loss or theft of their card and obtain an emergency card replacement, as a free service under the Thomas Cook MasterCard International Alliance.

Thomas Cook MasterCard Refund Centre (24-hour service – report loss or theft within 24 hours – tel: 05 90 83 30 (toll-free) or call collect: 44 17 33 50 29 95 (UK).

Accidents (Police secour) 17.
Ambulance 15 or **SAMU** 38 63 33 33.
Breakdown it is well-worth buying an AA 5-Star insurance policy to cover any serious breakdowns.
Chemist for emergency prescriptions, contact the local police station.
Dentist for emergency dental care, contact the local police station.
Doctor (SOS Médecins) 38 54 44 44 or 38 68 10 30.
Fire (Pompiers) 18.
Poisoning 47 66 15 15.

HEALTH AND INSURANCE

Up-to-date health advice can be obtained from all Thomas Cook branches.

France has no mandatory vaccination requirements, and no vaccination recommendations other than to keep tetanus and polio immunisation up to date. As in every other part of the world, AIDS is present.

All EU countries have reciprocal arrangements for reclaiming the costs of medical services. UK residents should obtain forms CM1 and E111 from any post office in the UK. This provides detailed information on how to claim and what is covered. Claiming is often a laborious and long drawn-out process and you are only covered for medical care, not for emergency repatriation, holiday cancellation, and so on. You are therefore strongly advised to take out a travel insurance policy to cover all eventualities. You can purchase such insurance through the AA, branches of Thomas Cook and most travel agents.

HOLIDAYS

1 January	New Year's Day
March/April	Easter Monday
1 May	Labour Day/May Day
8 May	VE Victory in Europe Day

LANGUAGE

Basic words and phrases

yes	oui
no	non
please	s'il vous plaît
thank you	merci
excuse me	excusez-moi
I am sorry	pardon
good morning	bonjour
good evening	bonsoir
good night	bonne nuit
goodbye	au revoir
I have...	j'ai...
It is...	c'est...
Do you speak English?	Parlez-vous anglais?
I do not understand	Je ne comprends pas.

Numbers and quantity

one	un	**six**	six
two	deux	**seven**	sept
three	trois	**eight**	huit
four	quatre	**nine**	neuf
five	cinq	**ten**	dix

a little	un peu
enough	assez
much/many	beaucoup
too much/many	trop

Charming house by the river at Bourges

May (mid)	Ascension Day
May (late)	Whit Monday
14 July	Bastille Day
15 August	Assumption Day
1 November	All Saints' Day
11 November	Remembrance Day (Armistice)
25 December	Christmas Day

Days of the week

Monday	lundi
Tuesday	mardi
Wednesday	mercredi
Thursday	jeudi
Friday	vendredi
Saturday	samedi
Sunday	dimanche

Months

January	janvier
February	février
March	mars
April	avril
May	mai
June	juin
July	juillet
August	août
September	septembre
October	octobre
November	novembre
December	décembre

when?	quand?
yesterday	hier
today	aujourd'hui
tomorrow	demain
at what time...?	à quelle heure...?
where is...?	où est...?
here	ici
there	là
near	près
before	avant
in front of	devant
behind	derrière
opposite	en face de
right	à droite
left	à gauche
straight on	tout droit
car park	un parking
petrol station	un poste à essence
parking prohibited	stationnement interdit
bridge	le pont
street	la rue
bus stop	l'arrêt du bus
underground station	la station de métro
railway station	la gare
platform	le quai
ticket office	le guichet
ticket	un billet
10 métro tickets	un carnet
single ticket	un aller simple

LOST PROPERTY

Report to the local police.
For lost or stolen credit cards ring
the following numbers:
American Express – tel: 47 77 70 07.
Diner's Club – tel: 47 62 75 00.
Visa – tel: 42 77 11 90.
Thomas Cook MasterCard Refund
Centre – tel: 05 90 83 30 (toll-free)
or (call collect) 44 17 33 50 29 95.

Eighteenth-century tapestry in the Château d'Ussé's central gallery

MEDIA
Newspapers
Regional newspapers are more influential than the national papers – *La Nouvelle République* is on sale everywhere. English-language dailies are available in larger towns.

Radio
FM radio stations offer a choice of non-stop classical music (Radio Classique), or pop. France Inter (LW 1892) is the equivalent of BBC Radio 4, which can itself sometimes be picked up in the region.

Television
France has four state-owned TV channels and two private ones, but many hotels now have satellite TV with a huge range of European and American channels on offer.

MONEY MATTERS
The French franc is the national currency. Each franc consists of 100 centimes. Credit cards are accepted almost everywhere. Thomas Cook MasterCard travellers' cheques free you from the hazards of carrying large amounts of cash, and in the event of loss or theft, can quickly be refunded (see emergency telephone number and emergency help locations page 183) French franc Eurocheques are widely accepted, and cheques denominated in other major currencies can be used, though the exchange rate can be unfavourable. In the major cities and towns, hotels, shops and restaurants

often accept travellers' cheques in lieu of cash.

MUSEUMS

National museums are closed on Tuesdays. They are free to students under 18. Reduced-price entry is charged for 18- to 25-year-olds and the over-60s. Municipal museums are usually closed on Mondays. Most museums close for lunch, except in July and August.

OPENING HOURS

Banks 8.30am–noon and 2–4pm weekdays; closed on either Saturday or Monday and at noon on the day before an official holiday.

Post offices 8am–7pm weekdays (until 5 or 6pm in smaller offices); 8am–noon Saturdays.

Food shops 7am–6.30 or 7.30pm; some open on Sunday mornings.

Other shops 9 or 10am–6.30 or 7.30pm; many are closed half or all day on Monday, and those in small towns and villages close from noon–2pm.

Hypermarkets open until 9pm or later, Monday to Saturday (some do not open until 2pm on a Monday).

SENIOR CITIZENS

Produce a passport to take advantage of any discounts, irrespective of whether or not you are a French national.

STUDENT ACCOMMODATION

There are 16 Auberges de Jeunesse (Youth Hostels) in the Loire Valley region. Contact the French headquarters for information: Fédération Unie des Auberges de Jeunesse, 27 rue Pajol, 75018 Paris. Tel: (1) 44 89 87 27 or (1) 46 47 00 01.

Senior citizens can claim discounts

TELEPHONES

Although coin-operated phone booths are common and need a handful of 1, 2 and 5-franc coins, the *télécarte* phone card is rapidly taking over. Buy one in a post office or *tabac* (tobacconists) to save time, trouble and money. The cards (50 francs and 120 francs) are much cheaper than a hotel call and simple to use.

Cheap rates operate between 10.30pm and before 8am, after 2pm on Saturday and all day Sunday. International calls are cheaper after 9pm.

There are only two regions in France: Paris and the provinces. To call any provincial number from anywhere in France, except Paris, simply dial the 8-figure number. To call Paris the 8-figure number has to be preceded by 161. To call a provincial number from Paris, the 8-digit number is preceded by 16.

To make an international call dial 19, then the country code (Australia: 61; Canada:1; Ireland: 353; New Zealand: 64; UK: 44; USA: 1).

TIME

The region is one hour ahead of GMT in winter and two hours ahead in summer. When it is noon in winter in Nantes or Orléans, it is:

9pm in Canberra, Australia
11am in Dublin, Ireland
11am in London, UK
6am in Ottawa, Canada
6am in Washington DC, USA
11pm in Wellington, New Zealand.

The local tourist office has up-to-date advice on what to see and do

Restaurant bills usually include all taxes and tips in the total

TIPPING

Cafés and restaurants include all taxes and tips on their bills. After an extended stay at a hotel, it is customary to leave a tip for the chambermaid. Porters, museum guides, taxi drivers and cinema usherettes always welcome a *pourboire* (tip).

TOILETS

There are public toilets in department stores, cafés and restaurants and there are self-cleaning *toilettes* (coin-operated booths) on the streets.

TOURIST OFFICES

For general information on the region contact:

Pays de la Loire CDT Pays de la Loire, 2 rue de la Loire, 44200 Nantes. Tel: 40 48 24 20 or 40 47 11 45; fax: 40 08 07 10.

Centre-Val-de-Loire CDT Centre-Val-de-Loire, 9 rue St-Pierre-Lentin, 45041 Orléans. Tel: 38 54 95 42; fax: 38 54 95 46.

TRAVELLERS WITH DISABILITIES

Access to the major tourist attractions is improving all the time. However, as most of the Loire's attractions are ancient castles and cathedrals, there are often real problems for wheelchair visitors. Although there are no overall guides for the region, the Comité National Français de Liaison pour la Réadaption des Handicapés (CNFLRH) does have leaflets (in French) on aspects of daily life in France.
38 boulevard Raspail; 75007 Paris.
Tel: (1) 45 58 90 13.

ACKNOWLEDGEMENTS
The Automobile Association would like to thank the following photographers, libraries and associations for their assistance in the preparation of this book.

COMITÉ RÉGIONAL DU TOURISME 150, 150/1, 159, 162, 163, 177a (E Milteau)
MARY EVANS PICTURE LIBRARY 8, 66a, 66b, 66c, 67a, 67b, 97a, 97b, 97c
FRENCH PICTURE LIBRARY 157
A LAURIOUX 44, 45a

The remaining pictures are held in the Association's own library (AA PHOTO LIBRARY) and were taken by R Moore with the exception of pages 4, 9, 18a, 35b, 39b, 40b, 49, 69a, 71, 75b, 86, 98, 107, 113, 126b, 127, 128, 135, 141b, 142a, 153, 173, 187, 188a which were taken by J Edmunson, pages 14, 83 taken by P Kenward, pages 7, 20a, 29b, 126a taken by B Smith and page 179 by R Strange.

The authors appreciate the help of Paul Ligtenberg and the Western Loire Tourist Board.

CONTRIBUTORS
Series adviser: Melissa Shales   **Designer:** Design 23   **Copy editor:** Christopher Catling
Verifier: Jenny Fry   **Indexer:** Marie Lorimer